Psychoanalytic Approaches to Sexual Problems

Psychoanalytic Approaches to Sexual Problems

Herbert S. Strean
Editor

The Haworth Press
New York

Psychoanalytic Approaches to Sexual Problems has also been published as *Current Issues in Psychoanalytic Practice,* Volume 1, Number 3, Fall 1984.

The Haworth Press, Inc., 28 East 22 Street, New York, NY 10010

Library of Congress Cataloging in Publication Data
Main entry under title:

Psychoanalytic approaches to sexual problems.

Also published as Current issues in psychoanalytic practice, vol. 1, no. 3. fall 1984.
Includes bibliographical references.
1. Psychosexual disorders. 2. Conflict (Psychology) 3. Psychoanalysis.
4. Psychotherapy. I. Strean, Herbert S. [DNLM: 1. Psychoanalytic Interpretation.
2. Sex Disorders. WM 460.5.S3 P974]
RC556.P744 1984 616.85'83 84-12961
ISBN 0-86656-341-5

Psychoanalytic Approaches to Sexual Problems

Current Issues in Psychoanalytic Practice
Volume 1, Number 3

CONTENTS

Psychoanalytic Approaches to Sexual Problems

A LETTER FROM THE EDITOR

Dear Reader,

Welcome to our issue on sexuality—a subject which intrigues us, stimulates us, and sometimes baffles us!

During the past decade, sexuality has "come out of the closet." People from all walks of life feel much freer than their forebears to bring their sexual conflicts and their sexual unhappiness to the helping professional. Yet, there is so much confusion on the part of therapists regarding the assessment and treatment of sexual problems. One frequent error made by many practitioners is to view sexuality as essentially a bodily experience without recognizing that the way individuals function sexually is very much related to how they like themselves and can love others. Often the practitioner fails to appreciate that people who cannot enjoy sex are plagued by anger, tortured by unacceptable fantasies, and cannot trust others.

The other oversight that we have seen among many helping professionals is the failure to realize that many presenting problems of our patients are really sexual problems. The man or woman who cannot succeed on the job is often very frightened of being sexually expressive and assertive. Frequently, marital arguments when studied carefully, turn out to be expressions of the partner's fears of sexual intimacy. Many children who have learning problems are really suffering from inhibitions in their sexual curiosity, and on and on!

We believe that this issue of our journal will go a long way to clarify many trouble spots for therapists as they try to help their patients enhance their sexual lives.

We trust that some of you will let us know how you feel about the articles in this issue. As a result of some of your comments, we are now planning to have a section for students who are in psychoanalytic training or are in some other kind of therapeutic training. Students should write to us about some of their concerns and we will try to devote a section of each issue of the journal to them. Perhaps you would like certain issues discussed or certain books examined? Let us know!

Best,

Herbert S. Strean
Editor

The Analytic Triad: A Contribution to the Theory of Transference

Reuben Fine

The theory of transference was set forth by Freud in a number of papers in the second decade. There the essential point was that the transference is made conscious to the patient by the analyst, and it is resolved by convincing him that in his transference-attitude he is reexperiencing emotional relations which had their origins in his earliest object attachments during the repressed period of his childhood (SE, XX, p. 42).

At the same time Freud maintained that transference is a universal phenomenon. In 1925 he wrote (XX, p. 42):

> Transference is merely uncovered and isolated by analysis. It is a universal phenomenon of the human mind, it decides the success of all medical influence, and in fact dominates the whole of each person's relation to his human environment.

Since transferences are found to all persons in the environment, the question naturally arises: what is the relationship between the transference or transferences to these other people and the transference to the analyst? And a corollary: suppose the transference to the analyst is resolved (a theoretical point of argument arises about whether this can really be done), what is the effect of such a resolution on the other transference(s) of the patient?

At another time, in *Group Psychology* (1921) Freud became more specific. There is always some other person who is important to the patient, or as Freud put it (XVIII, p. 69):

> In the individual's mental life someone else is invariably involved as a model, as an object, as a helper, as an opponent;

> and so from the very first individual psychology, in this extended but entirely justifiable sense of the words, is at the same time social psychology as well.

Thus putting these two statements together, there is for the analysand always the need to reconcile the two most important figures in his life: the analyst, and the important other person. For experience shows that it is almost always one other person who is the major transference figure outside the analysis, usually in the present, sometimes a person from the past. The analysis then revolves around the relative significance of these two transference figures. This is what I call the analytic triad. In practice every analyst knows that it is vital to resolve not only the transference to the analyst but also the transference to the other person, if that should be harmful to the individual in his life, which is often the case. Usually however less effort is directed toward resolving the other transference, unless it is blatantly destructive (and even then as we know many abrupt terminations are stimulated by the acting out of the transference to another person in a self-destructive way).

I

If we look for the childhood origins of the analytic triad, the first thought is to go back to the Oedipal situation. And of course the Oedipal conflict still plays a central role in all pathology.

But more recent investigation into the first year of life has revealed that a triadic situation is formed by the child much earlier, in some ways as early as the first week of life. Chiland (1982, p. 377), reviewing the infant literature, states: "The concept of a purely dyadic relationship between infant and mother is now as unacceptable as the concept of a stage of normal autism."

Thus she implies that Mahler's concept of a state of normal autism, like Freud's stage of primary narcissism, has to be abandoned in the light of newer findings. *The father is always present, somewhere in the background.* Even when he is absent, his absence makes itself felt. Andre Green writes (1975):

> (Since) there is no such thing as an infant because one never sees an infant without a crib, without arms holding it, without maternal care (Winnicott), we in turn may say that an infant

> with its mother does not exist. A mother-child couple does not exist without a father somewhere . . . Thus, we may state in the extreme that *there is no dyadic relationship.* (Chiland, 1982, pp. 368-369)

Among the luminous evidence she quotes to support the notion of an infant active and responsive from birth (and prenatally too in many respects, yet unresearched) is the following:

Imitation begins during the infant's first week of life. If the mother, or another adult, sticks out her tongue in front of the child, he begins to stick out his tongue. If the mother stops sticking out her tongue and bats her eyelashes, the baby bats his eyelashes. If she opens or closes her mouth, he does the same thing. Moreover, he synchronizes himself with her, and he seems to take pleasure in these games of reciprocal imitation.

As early as the age of twelve hours, newborn babies who hear recordings of spoken English, of isolated vocal sounds, of regular beating noises, and of spoken Chinese do not react to isolated vocal sounds or to beating noises, but move themselves synchronically with the structure of English and Chinese speech coming either from a recording or from a living person. At birth, babies turn their heads toward a clicking sound. They are not interested in pure sounds, but actively react to complex sounds and in particular to the high-pitched human voice.

They are sensitive to the smell of colostrum, and as early as the end of the first week (day six) they distinguish between a compress which has been in contact with their mother's breast and one which has been in contact with the breast of another nursing woman.

From birth on, there is an object-background discrimination, a reflex of fixation, and a visual pursuit under certain conditions. At the age of two weeks, babies recognize the face of the mother; they look at it more than at the face of a stranger through a kind of window placed above the crib. When the voice of the mother or of a stranger is produced by a loudspeaker, babies have a "gaze aversion" and turn away their heads if voice and face do not match.

One of Chiland's conclusions is (Chiland, 1982, p. 374):

> In the light of the data obtained during the past 10 years, it seems clear that "normal autism" is a poorly chosen term for the description of the infant during the first months of life. We can see that his perceptions are in the service of the discovery

and the recognition of the mother and of the interaction with her.

A mass of confirmatory evidence of these propositions is provided by Lichtenberg in his recent book (1983). His overall summary is (Lichtenberg, 1983, pp. 44-45):

> We have already seen that human infants begin extrauterine life with demonstrable functional capacities. Rather than being amorphous organisms, beset by hunger and molded by the mother, infants show a lawful order of their functioning, with five organized behavioral states: alert wakefulness, quiescent wakefulness, REM sleep, NREM sleep and crying . . . . From birth on, in the full-term baby, these states organize the neonate's life in temporal sequences, in conjunction with the stimuli of the extrauterine environment.

Thus this new material indicates that some differentiation between mother and father takes place from birth on. One might stretch a point, as Melanie Klein once did, by saying that the Oedipal conflict starts at birth. However, this would ignore the development of the ego. It seems clear that while some differentiation exists from birth on, as the ego grows, it handles the differences in ever more advanced ways. While this process still may be seen to culminate in the classical Oedipal conflict, the long pre-history of that conflict must now be taken into consideration in both theory and practice.

Much attention has been devoted in recent years to the period from fifteen months to three years. Greenspan (1980, 1982) has suggested the term "dyadic-phallic stage of development" to describe the early phallic stage, somewhere between Mahler's rapprochement phase and the classical Oedipal period. During this stage, the father's role is especially unique in helping the child to stabilize basic ego functions such as reality testing, impulse regulation, mood stabilization, delineation of self from others, and focussed concentration.

Greenspan delineates a number of stages of development: 1) homeostasis; 2) forming a human attachment; 3) somatopsychological differentiation; 4) behavioral organization, initiative and internalization; 5) forming mental representations and finally 6) the dyadic-phallic stage of development. Although he particularly emphasizes the role of the father in the dyadic-phallic stage, he stipulates a role for the father at each previous stage as well.

Herzog (1982) coined the term "father hunger," and felt that the father's role was primarily that of the modulation of aggressive drive and fantasy. He and his group studied children whose fathers were absent, either completely or partially, because of divorce. A striking feature of these children's productions at all developmental stages was the predominance of aggressive themes and content. A second striking difference was the predominance of aggressive motives in boys thus bereft between the ages of eighteen and sixty months. Later on (between the ages of sixty and eighty-four months) little girls begin to be represented in equal numbers. These observations led to the hypothesis that a specific role is played by the male parent in the modulation of aggressive-drive fantasy in the young child, and that the father's absence at this time may have specific and long-range consequences. A second hypothesis was that little boys are more vulnerable or at least feel more vulnerable to disruptions in the control of aggressive drives and fantasy than are their female counterparts, at least until the age of five years. Little boys therefore suffer more when family disruption leads to father loss.

To describe the affective state and longing experienced by father-deprived children, Greenspan introduces the notion of "father-hunger." However, he does not consider the possibility that a good part of the aggression displayed by these boys, and some of the longing, may occur by identification with the abandoned mother, who usually is filled with resentment and hatred of the absent father, even when she herself has initiated the separation. I have elsewhere (Fine, 1975) hypothesized that an essential part of the intensity of the Oedipal situation is an identification with the hostility of the partner of the opposite sex, so that, e.g., the boy's anger at the father derives from the mother's hatred of the father, as well as from other psychological and biological sources.

In any case, it is already clear that a triadic situation exists for the child from birth on, that this triadic situation grows and changes with the maturing ego of the child, and that it is strongly affected by the emotional reactions of the parents to the child, to one another and to the outside world. This could serve then as the infantile origins of the analytic triad.

Such an assumption expands the classical image of a two-person symbiosis, primarily between the child and the mother, which is then recapitulated in the analytic situation as a transference. Just as the relationship with the mother cannot be properly understood without reference to the father, the transference to the analyst cannot be properly understood without reference to the important third party involved.

II

As is well known, Freud had no confidence in the treatment of the relatives. Quite the contrary; he saw them as expressing an "unavoidable" opposition to psychoanalytic treatment, and even warned against giving them any literature to read. He concluded (XII, p. 120):

> As regards the treatment of their "relatives" [this word is put in quotation marks for some reason; the quotation marks are omitted by Strachey] I must confess myself utterly at a loss, and I have in general little faith in any individual treatment of them.

This attitude toward the relatives (and other close persons) has changed considerably in the course of the years. Today it is customary, at least in large cities where plenty of analysts are available, to routinely refer the relatives for therapy or analysis to some other analyst (some may prefer to see the relatives themselves, as for instance Freud did with the betrothed of Ernest Jones, Loe Kann [Brome, 1983]). Various possibilities may then develop. A common problem stemming from the separation of analysts is that the battle between, say spouses, becomes a battle between analysts, each analyst taking the side of whichever spouse he or she is treating. In a few cases they have even appeared in court on behalf of the spouse they are treating. The extension of analysis to the broader segments of the population, especially those who are culturally normal, has played an important role in this development. It may be noted here that Ernest Jones, when he first came across Melanie Klein, sent his children to her for analysis, convinced (as most analysts were at that time and still are) that the normal process of growing up leaves all kinds of scars which can effectively be modified or erased by analytic treatment (Brome, 1983, pp. 154-155).

Classically, Freud stressed the centrality of the transference, and its concomitant resistance. In 1912 he wrote (SE, XII, p. 108):

> It is on that field (transference) that the victory must be won—the victory whose expression is the permanent cure of the neurosis. It cannot be disputed that controlling the phenomena of transference presents the psychoanalyst with the greatest difficulties. But it should not be forgotten that it is precisely they that do us the inestimable service of making the patient's hidden and forgotten erotic impulses immediate and manifest. For when all is said and done, it is impossible to destroy anyone *in absentia* or *in effigie.*

In the ensuing years a voluminous literature has developed about how to handle the transference properly. While certain general principles are commonly observed, such as the preservation of analytic neutrality, and the avoidance of social relations, in general the analysis of the transference has remained an art rather than a science. In 1972 Bird wrote: "Nothing about analysis is less well known than how individual analysts actually use transference in their day-to-day work with patients" (Bird, 1972, p. 271).

In spite of the importance attached to transference by Freud, Gill has recently argued that Freud did not make it important enough. In Gill's 1982 monograph he writes (Gill, 1982, p. 177):

> The point of this monograph is to argue that the analysis of the transference should play a greater and more central role in analytic technique than I believe it does in prevailing practice. The development of the analysis of the transference took place early in Freud's work, and although his use of it doubtlessly grew in sophistication and centrality, I believe it never became as central as it should be. Freud remained of the view that the analysis of the transference is ancillary to the analysis of the neurosis rather than contending that the analysis of the neurosis should take place essentially by way of the transference.

In spite of his strictures against his contemporary fellow analysts, what Gill sets forth in his monograph is essentially a programmatic approach. He does not consider, or at least does not consider in any detail, the innumerable variations which occur in practice, the many ways in which the analysand reacts to the transference, the innumerable resistances that come up, nor what the reactions of the analysands are to pure transference analysis, of the kind that he urges.

What he leaves out in other words is all the details of technique (Fine, 1982).

Although Langs has recently propounded an idiosyncratic theory of his own, to the effect that many of the analysand's supposed transference reactions are more the consequences of the analyst's incorrect interventions, especially in the first year, in his more comprehensive discussion of the literature on transference Langs (1976) came to a somewhat more sober conclusion. There he wrote (Langs, 1976, p. 19):

> Freud created an ingenious foundation for the study not only of the psychoanalytic but of all therapeutic relationships, and his writings on this subject have spawned a massive and convoluted literature, striking still for its many unresolved issues.

Among these many unresolved issues a central one is the connection between the real relationship and the transference. The significance of this real relationship was particularly stressed by Greenson (1967, 1971). His position was that the successful outcome of an analysis depends more on the real relationship than on anything else; this goes together with his concept of the working alliance. Greenson states that for the full flowering and ultimate resolution of the patient's transference reactions, it is essential in all cases to acknowledge, clarify, differentiate, and even nurture the nontransference or relatively transference-free reactions between patient and analyst. The technique of "only analyzing" or "only interpreting" transference phenomena may stifle the development and clarification of the transference neurosis and act as an obstacle to the actualization of the transference-free or "real" reactions of the patient.

There can be no question about the centrality of interpreting the transference, Greenson says, but it is also important to deal with the nontransference interactions between patient and analyst. This may require noninterpretative or nonanalytic interventions, but these approaches are very different from analytic procedures, including such techniques as reassurance, suggestion, or intervention in the patient's life.

Similarly Leo Stone (1961) in his famous book, *The Analytic Situation,* while in general adhering to the classical posture of neutrality, warned against the analyst's excessive adherence to it. Total silence may create the danger of undue regression in the patient and may generate impairments in the unfolding of the transference neurosis. Stone believes that finding the analyst to be human even when revelations reflect technical errors is less detrimental to the analysis than stiff, inconsiderate, unreal attitudes and practices. In advocating acknowledgement of selective facts about the analyst, Stone suggested that the facts serve as a reasonable corrective or measuring rod for distorted information that supports transference resistances rather than the therapeutic alliance.

The theoretical assumption, going back to Freud, has always been that if the patient can develop a suitable transference neurosis, he can be analyzed. Considerable doubt about this general proposition has been expressed through the years, and numerous variations have been suggested to improve the outcome. Yet when all was said and done, the fact-finding commission of the American Psychoanalytic Association, which labored on the task for almost twenty years, could come to no definitive conclusions (Hamburg et al., 1967). And in the most recent attempt at a summary, Bachrach (1983) can only emphasize the high degree of individuality of the psychoanalytic enterprise, analysis of transference or not. In his summation he writes (Bachrach, 1983, p. 201):

> there is, and always has been, considerable individuality in the understanding and application of the psychoanalytic procedure; this individuality raises questions about the often assumed comparability of clinical observation and data; and this individuality must be taken into consideration in a realistic understanding of the factors that govern analyzability . . . . a deepening of our understanding requires systematic inquiry into individual differences, including the contribution of the analyst to the development of the analytic process

Because of the high degree of individuality, the analysis of the transference alone is not likely, without consideration of other factors, to yield uniform and uniformly satisfactory results. It serves as a guideline, indispensable in its way, but not the only guideline to the conduct of a successful analysis.

III

Another factor which must be considered in the transference is the *triad,* i.e., the relationship between the transference to the analyst and the transference to the most significant other person in the patient's life. This aspect of the transference situation has been largely ignored (e.g., Gill does not even mention it).

One of the few authors who has devoted extensive consideration to the analytic triad (although in another form and another context) is Michael Balint in his book *The Basic Fault* (1968). In the basic fault position, two and only two people are involved; the patient does not have the capacity to move on to the Oedipal situation. Clinically it shows up in the difference between the benign and malignant forms of regression. In benign regression, which is one of the cornerstones of the classical analytic technique, the characteristic features are (Balint, 1968, p. 146):

1. not much difficulty in establishing a mutually trusting, *arglos,* unsuspecting relationship, which is reminiscent of the primary relationship toward primary substances;
2. a regression, leading to a true new beginning, and ending in a real new discovery;
3. the regression is for the sake of recognition, in particular, of the patient's internal problems;
4. only moderately high intensity of the demands, expectations or "needs;"
5. absence of signs of severe hysteria in the clinical symptomatology and of genital-orgastic elements in the regressed transference.

On the other hand, the malignant regression shows the following characteristic features:

1. since the mutually trusting relationship is highly precariously balanced, the *arglos,* unsuspecting, atmosphere breaks down repeatedly, and frequently symptoms of desperate clinging develop as safeguards and reassurance against another possible breakdown;
2. a malignant form of regression, several unsuccessful attempts at reaching a new beginning, a constant threat of an unending spiral of demands or needs, and of development of addiction-like states;
3. the regression is aimed at gratification by external action;
4. suspiciously high intensity of demands, expectations or "needs,"
5. presence of signs of severe hysteria in the clinical picture, and

> of genital-orgastic elements both in the normal and in the regressed form of transference.

Balint attributed the malignant form of regression to a deficit in the child's upbringing. He saw the patient as subsisting in a state where he always demands unconditional love in a two-person relationship; in more ordinary language, he remains an infant fixated on the mother and never moves on. Hence the regression in the analysis symbolizes a return to mother from which the patient never recovers.

Others, particularly those who have concerned themselves with schizophrenia, have naturally made similar observations. In all these cases, there is a fundamental dispute about whether the regressed (schizophrenic) individual suffers from some inherent defect or deficit which prevents him from going out to the world, or whether it is a state induced by an overpowering mother who simply will not let the child grow up, so he adjusts himself to this mother and never goes beyond her.

This argument, about deficit or traumatic early experience, can be found all along the line in psychology and psychoanalysis. The deficit theory assumes some organic basis for the inability to grow up. Some analysts have likewise postulated a deficit, presumably of an organic nature. Thus Mahler (1968) viewed the psychotic child as one who is unable to benefit from mother's love, rather than one who is crushed by a destructive mother. Stolorow and Lachmann (1980) also stress the difference between deficit and regression. Kohut (1977) speaks of the primary disturbances of the self, of which he enumerates five (Kohut, 1977, pp. 192-193): 1) psychosis; 2) borderline states; 3) schizoid and paranoid personalities; 4) narcissistic personality disorders and 5) narcissistic behavior disorders (e.g., perversion, delinquency or addiction). Although he does not overtly commit himself to an etiology of early mother-child disturbance or organic defect, since he uses the term "primary disturbances" and since he regards the first three above as unanalyzable, he seems to be inclined to accept the hypothesis of some organic or hereditary defect.

To try to resolve this question would take us too far afield, especially into the area of the etiology of schizophrenia. There is evidence for an hereditary factor in schizophrenia, but there is equally a great deal of evidence for the significance of the "horrible" childhood of which Bleuler (1978) speaks. The significance of the analytic triad would apply most strongly to those patients whose disturbance is psychogenic in origin.

IV
CASE MATERIAL

Some case material will now be presented in order to clarify how the use of the concept of the analytic triad leads to greater theoretical clarity, and to greater therapeutic effectiveness.

1. *The Case of Dora.* We can begin appropriately with some of Freud's cases (Kanzer and Glenn, 1980; Jones, 1953-1957). With Dora, the eighteen-year-old young woman who left treatment abruptly, Freud took himself to task for missing the negative transference. The triad that Freud described was that of himself, Dora and Herr K. He interpreted, after the analysis ended, her abrupt termination to acting out the revenge on him that she felt toward Herr K. In the case history he writes (SE, VII, p. 119):

> But I was deaf to the first note of warning, thinking I had ample time before me, since no further stages of transference developed and the material for the analysis had not yet run dry. In this way the transference took me unawares, and because of the unknown quantity in me which reminded Dora of Herr K., she took her revenge on me as she wanted to take her revenge on him, and deserted me as she believed herself to have been deceived and deserted by him. Thus she *acted out* an essential part of her recollections and phantasies instead of reproducing them in the treatment . . . . When it is possible to work transferences into the analysis at an early stage, the course of the analysis is retarded and obscured, but its existence is better guaranteed against sudden and overwhelming resistances.

Freud later tells us that fifteen months after termination Dora came back for more treatment. "One glance at her face, however, was enough to tell me that she was not in earnest over her request" (SE, VII, p. 121). The reasoning behind this feeling of Freud's is not given. He did not take her back, she married (exactly when, it is not said) and, according to Freud, tore herself free from her father and was reclaimed once more by the realities of life (p. 122).

However, a paper by Felix Deutsch (1957) provides much more relevant information about what happened to Dora subsequent to the eleven weeks' treatment. Deutsch saw her medically in 1922, twenty-four years after treatment with Freud had terminated. Her hostility toward men had remained undiminished. She accused her husband of unfaithfulness, and was angry at her son because he had started going out with girls. Her love life was frustrated; she was frigid. Tearfully, she denounced men in general as selfish, demanding, and ungiving.

Then she flirtatiously asked Deutsch whether he was an analyst. She then revealed to him that she was Dora, that she took pride in being a famous case, and that she had never seen an analyst since leaving Freud. Her marriage was horrible. She was full of symptoms; eventually she died of cancer of the colon. She had been, according to Deutsch's informant, "one of the most repulsive hysterics" he had ever met.

Thus looked at retrospectively, Dora's improvement was merely a transference reaction, and led to no permanent alteration in her character structure. She remained in transference to Freud because she knew that she had become a famous case; now she seemed to love Freud (because he had made her famous) and hated her husband, a new triad. Possibly because of the transference to Freud, and his later rejection of her, she never returned to treatment.

The history indicates that there was another transference Freud had completely overlooked: the transference to her future husband. This was the girl that said in effect (SE, VII, p. 120): "Men are all so detestable that I would rather not marry. This is my revenge." Her subsequent marriage was then an act of revenge, both against Freud and against her husband. The triad of Freud-Dora-husband was firmly established, and she lived it out for the rest of her life. Freud was so engrossed in the love affair with Herr K. (and also her homosexual feelings for Frau K.) that he did not pay any attention to her relationships with marriageable young men of her age, although it was by no means unusual in the Vienna of that day for an eighteen-year-old girl to marry.

2. *The Wolf Man.* An interesting postscript to the case of the Wolf Man is now available, in a book by Karin Obholzer, a Viennese journalist, who befriended him late in life, and wrote about her interviews (Obholzer, 1982). He has also been extensively described by others; the reports are gathered in the book *The Wolf Man by The Wolf Man* (1971).

When he came into analysis with Freud, the Wolf Man had a woman he wanted to marry, Therese, and whom he later did marry.

Thus a triad existed from the very beginning of the analysis. In fact, intuitively the Wolf Man appreciated Freud's acceptance of his love, and saw it as one inducement to go to Freud rather than some other psychiatrist. He writes (Wolf Man, 1958, pp. 348-352):

> The error of "classical" psychiatry had been that, ignorant of the existence and laws of the unconscious, it derived everything from the physical . . . . Everything the neurotic undertook was considered sick. If, for example, he fell in love with a woman, this was described as "manic," or as a "compulsion." But for Freud the "break-through to the woman" would under certain circumstances be considered a healthy achievement, a sign of the neurotic's will to live, an attempt at restitution.

Therese was a nurse in one of the sanatoriums that the Wolf Man had stayed in. In his own evaluation of her before the relationship started, the Wolf Man wrote (Wolf Man, p. 50):

> My own impression of Therese, as well as everything I had heard about her, made me conclude that she was a woman who would avoid any amorous involvement and that she would be particularly disinclined to enter into a relationship with a patient of the institution which employed her.

This emotional coldness never was brought into the analysis with Freud, nor for that matter with any of the other analysts he saw after Freud. Obholzer relates that the Wolf Man was in analysis all his life, on and off, and that he was maintained as a "prize specimen" by a number of analysts, a position that he both enjoyed and resented (Obholzer, 1982).

As is known, Therese committed suicide when the Nazis took over Austria, although as a German Aryan she was in no personal danger. After she died, the Wolf Man went from one woman to another, usually apparently only for sexual purposes. Eventually, in his later years he attached himself to a woman named Luise (Obholzer, 1982, p. 223) whom he both loved and despised, the same ambivalent transference he had to Freud. When Obholzer began to interview him, he eventually began to make a play for her, saying (Obholzer, 1982, p. 217): "You would be the right woman for me." Thus the kind of triad that he had with Freud, a warm understanding father figure, coupled with a cold demanding woman, was never broken.

The ambivalence about Freud is brought out by Miss Obholzer in the Wolf Man's statement that in 1919, when Freud analyzed him free of charge, and even collected money for him, he was primarily interested in getting back to Odessa, where he thought he could still salvage some of his fortune. He resented Freud bitterly for preventing him from doing so.

The relationship with women was analyzed in terms of its childhood roots, both psychological and otherwise. Freud's management of the affair with Therese was certainly rather odd by modern standards. At first he insisted that there should be no marriage during the analysis. This is an ordinary rule, but led to a constant demand by the Wolf Man that he should be allowed to marry. Evidently he thought Freud was annoyed by this constant preoccupation. At one point, he says, Freud raised his hands above his head and cried out pathetically: "For twenty-four hours now I have not heard the sacred name Therese!" (Wolf Man, 1971, p. 85).

Finally, shortly before the end of the treatment in 1914, he and Therese visited Freud together. Freud remarked that she "looked like a czarina" (p. 90) and was pleased by her reserved and serious nature. So he gave the marriage his full approval. Obviously the transference to Therese (the mother-nurse), which would be everyday food for an analysis nowadays, was never touched by Freud. As a result, the Wolf Man spent the rest of his life seeking out unresponsive women. It would certainly not be appropriate to criticize Freud for a stage in the development of his psychoanalytic technique. But it is appropriate to point out that even the most detailed analysis of childhood, as with Dora and the Wolf Man, may not be sufficient to influence the present-day realities of the love relationships or transferences. (That all love involves a greater or lesser degree of transference may automatically be assumed [Fine, 1984].)

3. *The Homosexual Girl.* The patient, to whom Freud did not give a name, was an eighteen-year-old girl in love with a woman many years older than herself. Freud's handling of this case is surprising and instructive, especially in the light of what has happened since.

It was only after an attempt at suicide that she agreed at the urging of her parents to consult Freud. After some preliminary investigation, Freud felt that the transference was too negative, and recommended that she should be analyzed by a woman. Whether or not the parents followed this advice we are not told (SE, XVIII, p. 164).

However, upon closer examination, the case history raises many questions. In the first place, while the title of the paper is "A Case of Homosexuality in a Woman," we are surprised to find that the girl was not overtly homosexual. "With none of the objects of her adoration had the patient enjoyed anything beyond a few kisses and embraces; her genital chastity, if one may use such a phrase, had remained intact" (p. 153). Today we would certainly say that she was bisexual.

Freud traced the girl's homosexual leanings to the birth of a brother when she was sixteen years old. This aroused such strong resentment against the father that she wished to repudiate all men. However this too is contradicted by Freud. Her dreams revealed the desire to be a mother, and to have men's love. "She did not conceal from me that she meant to marry, but only in order to escape from her father's tyranny and to follow her true inclinations undisturbed" (p. 165). Further, she said, one could easily have sexual relations with a man and a woman at one and the same time.

She is thus expressing her ambivalence about becoming a sexual woman. At one point Freud did something very peculiar, in much the same way that he had refused to take Dora back (it will be recalled that Dora also wanted to marry in order to take revenge on men). "Warned through some slight impression or other, I told her one day that I did not believe these dreams, that I regarded them as false or hypocritical, and that she intended to deceive me just as she habitually deceived her father" (p. 165). Thus Freud repeated in his countertransference exactly what the parents had done with the birth of her brother: as soon as the feminine sexual wishes came to the fore, he rejected them as a "deception" thus in effect branding her a homosexual. It was not the girl who was rejecting him; it was Freud who was rejecting the girl.

A further oddity of the case history is that the society lady the girl pursued, ten years older than the patient, was not really a homosexual but also bisexual: she lived with a woman with whom she had sex, while at the same time she carried on promiscuous affairs with a number of men. By identifying with such a woman, the patient was really expressing her wish to let go sexually, a wish that every adolescent girl has. The same wish came out later in her fantasy of having sex with a man and a woman after marriage. But Freud was so intent on seeing her as a homosexual that he totally ignored this aspect of her budding sexuality as well.

The conceptualization of the triad would have brought the patient much deeper into the analysis, or at least might have, instead of Freud's cold repudiation of her. On the one hand she had a negative transference to Freud in the beginning, on the other she was in love with the coquette who was bisexual and promiscuous with men. Such a triad is by no means unanalyzable, as we know from our every day experience. The initial negative transference could be understood just as well in seeing Freud as a sexually prohibitive father, a role he actually played out. Had he played a sexually permissive role, the negative transference might well have been resolved.

Thus, once more it is only with the full understanding of the analytic triad that the total transference situation can be properly grasped and worked out.

The following examples are taken from my own practice.

4. *Harriet,* a twenty-seven-year-old married woman with two small children, sought me out to announce that she was going to divorce her husband and move to California. Had she really wished to do that, there was no need to consult an analyst. I suggested that she try analysis. The second session, she came back to say that she was willing to enter analysis, and had called off her trip to California.

Harriet was the heiress to a large fortune. In her teens she had been extremely promiscuous, as a result of which her grandfather, the source of the family wealth, had cut her out of his will. In retaliation she married a man old enough to be her father, who also had some severe physical handicaps, and was unsuitable as a husband and in many other ways.

After a few years of this unhappy marriage, and two children, Harriet wanted out. She recognized the terrible mistake she had made. But to leave the marriage, she needed someone else's support. Hence she came to me to set up a triad: the man she could love and the man she could hate. When her husband in turn demanded a financial settlement to end the marriage, that sealed her decision.

But the relationship with the analyst was not easy for her to manage. Her self-hatred was extreme, further fueled by a bitter fight with her near-psychotic mother, and by some severe somatic problems of her own. She felt that she was not good enough for the analyst. Consequently, once the marriage had been dissolved, she promptly took a lover who was, as in the story books, the family chauffeur. As she put it, her solution was "one for show and one for blow." As we would put it more scientifically, she could not sustain the analysis without a triadic situation; if she had not taken a lover, and especially one who was as obviously unsuitable as her husband, she would have been psychologically unable to continue the analysis.

Eventually the affair with the lover broke up as well. There followed more lovers, as she went through the vicissitudes of the transference. Each one provided a new analytic triad, which was analyzed: the lover on the one hand provided actual gratification, on the other hand he served as protection against the feelings about the analyst. As these triads were successfully analyzed, she eventually saw their transference implications, gave them up and was able to make a much happier marriage. She also discovered some untapped artistic talent in herself, which she unexpectedly brought to a professional level. (A similar case is described in my book *The Intimate Hour* [1979] as "Holly, the Abandoned Woman.")

5. *Alice,* a twenty-seven-year-old school teacher, came to analysis because of painful intercourse and an unhappy marital situation. She too had a lover in addition to her husband, but the affair was unsatisfactory to her. She specifically stated that one of her main reasons for coming to analysis was to be able to leave her husband: thus again a triad, with positive feelings toward one man, negative toward another. Shortly after the analysis began she was able to separate. She also broke off the affair because her lover was married and began to date a number of other men.

None of these men meant much to her. One night she woke up at 2:00 a.m. with a lover in her bed, flew into a violent temper tantrum, and kicked him out (behavior most unlike her at other times).

Outwardly positive, deep negative feelings also surfaced in the transference. Her sessions were held on Monday, Wednesday and Friday. For quite a while before every Friday session she would take a drink, then come and let me have the brunt of her anger.

Alice's problems were primarily Oedipal. She was the daughter of intellectualized over-controlled parents who had however always been loving and devoted to her. In fact, as she described herself, her problem was that she was always too well adjusted. The dyspareunia, as well as her constant search for new lovers, revealed that her conflicts lay primarily in the genital sphere. Actually no severe oral or anal traumatic material ever surfaced, but the Oedipal memories and conflicts were quite strong.

The transference never became too intense, unlike that of Harriet, and Marie (to be described below). But an unexpected incident in my life brought the recognition that her feelings about me must be deeper than she realized. She knew that my wife was pregnant, since home and office were in the same apartment. When my wife went into labor, a notice was pasted on the door asking the patients to keep their next regular appointment. She suspected what had happened, went to a bakery shop and bought some cake to "console" herself. Consciously she accepted the birth of the baby (a girl) with equanimity, although a good deal of the analysis had centered around the rivalry with her younger brother, born when she was four years old.

One year later, she was still coming on the same days. Almost to the day my daughter was born the patient announced that she might be pregnant. Since there was a realistic possibility, the fear was not analyzed until she called in before the next session to announce that it was a false alarm. I then pointed out to her that the false pregnancy occurred almost a year to the day after my daughter had been born.

Here too the transference has to be understood in terms of the triadic situation. This incident was quite obviously a recapitulation of the birth of her brother; my wife and I were mother and father.

However, the event, although thoroughly analyzed, had unexpected consequences. Shortly after, she announced that she was terminating analysis because of a preconceived time table that she had never before revealed, which stipulated that she was to complete analysis, take a trip to Europe and then get married.

She literally acted out the time table. Once analysis was completed, she went to Europe. Upon her return she married, a good marriage to a man very much like her beloved father. Then she had a baby and moved to a street near the analyst's apartment. (Incidentally, such geographic proximity has not been uncommon in my practice, although it has rarely been mentioned in the literature. One patient of mine actually moved into the same building, where he stayed until the analysis was concluded.)

5. *Marie,* an unmarried nineteen-year-old student, had no sooner sat down to face the analyst than she asked: "Are you married?" This of course was handled analytically. Three sessions later she terminated abruptly and married a Yugoslav with whom she had been living for some time. Six months after, she began to have homosexual nightmares, at which point she returned for some real analysis.

In such a situation, by no means unusual, one could interpret the marriage as an acting out of the Oedipal wishes, or as a negative reaction to the analyst because he would not give her direct gratification. What I am suggesting is that it is most fruitful to do neither, but to see her behavior as the interplay of two transferences. After her marriage, the transference to the husband became negative, partly because he was of the old-fashioned school and would have none of this psychology "pap," and partly because her childhood conflicts were totally unresolved. The transference to the analyst became positive, of the idealizing type.

Marie had suffered from lifelong anxieties. When a young child during WWII, she was terrified to go out in the street because bombs might hit her (air raid warnings were posted in her home town). Later in camp, when she was about ten, she became a bully and forced the younger girls to sit on a home-made potty until they defecated. When she graduated from high school with high honors, her father, then terminally ill, warned her, "From now on it's down." During the course of Marie's treatment, her mother once wrote the analyst accusing him of malpractice, stating that Marie should give up her job (by now she was a teacher, functioning reasonably well) and come home to Mama, where she would be well sheltered.

The powerful erotic transference that ensued should also be seen as the complement of the hostile rejection by the parents, and the incessant attacks on analysis by her husband. Although he had once attempted suicide, by and large he lived on a plane of cultural denial. Thus again the theoretical formulation should be in terms of the two transferences, to the analyst and to the husband, rather than in terms of the one, the erotic element.

Marie's analysis was a stormy one. About a year after she began, she separated from her husband; the marriage was obviously a bad one. She then began to date various men. But at one point the analyst suddenly observed that she had not been going out for a long time. When he called this to her attention, she confirmed it, saying that she had not had a date for a year. Asked for the reason, she said that the analyst had forgotten the agreement that they had made, that if she did not go out with anybody, he would not either. Naturally no such agreement had been made; it was her fantasy of marrying the analyst in not too disguised a form.

One of her lifelong fantasies had been to spend six months in one country and then go on to another country. When the marriage to the analyst did not materialize for the second time, she acted out this fantasy and went off to Mexico. Here she learned the language, and functioned well. The triad here was positive toward the distant analyst, negative to the young men she dated in Mexico. After about a year, she again returned to analysis.

The analysis did not end satisfactorily. She made a considerable amount of progress, but the demand for marriage with the analyst persisted, almost unabated. Again the transference to other young men in her environment was largely idealized and negative. At one point she joined a group, against the analyst's wishes. Here she met a young man of thirty who was still a virgin. She offered to be his first sex partner (the group leader permitted outside contacts), which he accepted. To her it meant "nothing"; actually it was a way of seducing and rejecting a man. He in turn went into a long homosexual period after sex with her.

Eventually she made a better marriage than the first, and left analysis. However, many of her conflicts remained unresolved. But the marriage may again be seen as part of a triad: positive but unfulfilled physically with the analyst, negative but with physical gratification by the husband.

6. *Beverly,* a forty-five-year-old woman in a full-blown schizophrenic episode, was being seen daily, seven times a week. She was delusional; e.g., she thought that she caused electrical machinery to stop, which limited her activities severely. There were several repetitive hallucinations; e.g., she thought that police cars drove up to her and said, "Clink you."

Beverly had a number of schizophrenic episodes before the present one, and had been to about ten different psychiatrists in the course of a dozen years, with three hospitalizations, shock treatment (this was in the days before the tranquilizers) and intensive psychotherapy several times. There were remissions but nothing seemed to help permanently.

Before she came to see me, she had been in treatment with a psychiatrist she adored. He was young, handsome, and born not too far from her home town. But she was not aware of his problems. He was the son of a judge and as such fancied himself something of a lawyer. Accordingly, he arranged a divorce for her while she was hospitalized, and took over the management of her affairs in other ways.

The triad that she set up with him, the first psychiatrist who really offered her any help, was positive with him, and negative with her husband. The negative transference to her husband was accentuated by the fact that when he came back from France after WWII, he announced he had fallen in love with a French woman and wanted a divorce. On her psychiatrist's advice she acceded.

Unknown to her, however, the psychiatrist began to dabble in drugs. Since he did not have a narcotics license (he was still a resident) he began to forge prescriptions on the blanks of some of his hospital colleagues who did. Caught, he fled to another country, giving her only three days notice to transfer to another therapist. The shock, coupled with her husband's demand for a divorce, set her off on another psychotic episode. This began with a dream: "I touch my cousin, and the shock kills him." She also began a frantic, totally unrealistic attempt to move.

The transference to me was largely negative for a long time. She was convinced that she would ruin my practice, and when she occasionally heard some people talking in the back of my apartment (my family lived there) she felt that somebody was raising a ruckus to get me out.

Predominantly the negative transference took the form of the repetitious question: How can I really trust you? This in turn was coupled with a request for a third person: if only she could meet someone who knew me she would be able to have more confidence in me. Here was another triad: the distant substitute therapist toward whom she could be positive, the analyst toward whom she was negative.

When I went on a summer vacation I did switch her to another analyst for the period that I was away. In fact, the transference to him was positive (but still negative toward me—she blamed me for some of her symptoms). When I returned she expressed great pleasure in the switch, and stated that she could now trust me more because I had such nice friends.

Eventually she calmed down, got over the psychotic symptoms, and lived out the normal life of an aging woman. But one further triad developed. She went back to work at her former skill in a publishing house. Here her immediate superior was an attractive young woman. The patient had had some homosexual experience in her adolescence, then given it up at twenty to get married. This young supervisor rearoused her homosexuality, and she became convinced that the woman was in love with her. When the analyst questioned this, she became furious at him. The situation became so disturbing that the supervisor asked for an appointment with the analyst to decide the best way to let her go. By that time Beverly was well into her fifties, had a small income from her ex-husband, and decided to retire. The analysis stopped at this point, though she was encouraged to come back whenever she felt the need, which she did several times. The later sessions were all supportive, and no further inner changes in her occurred.

7. The case of *Frank,* a sixty-five-year-old man who was in analysis with a series of analysts for a period of almost forty years, could serve to provide a different theoretical approach to the interminable patient, one of the great bugaboos of all analysts.

Frank was one of six children. When his mother became ill, the children were placed in an orphanage (this was in the 1920s when foster care scarcely existed). Although she recovered in about a year, it was decided that he should stay at the orphanage until he was eighteen.

Upon discharge, he went home. But he felt an enormous sense of shame at being home. His mother was allegedly a typhoid carrier, so that he could not invite any of his friends to the house. His father was a Talmudic scholar who at first made a living from a pushcart on the east side, then later became a toilet attendant in one of the large hotels.

WWII was probably the happiest time of Frank's life. He saw service overseas, and was rapidly promoted. Though offered a permanent military appointment, he preferred civilian life.

Upon discharge he felt crippled by anxieties, and sought out an analyst. At that time he had never formed any significant romantic attachment. To the first analyst he made a strongly positive transference in the beginning, then bogged down in endless carping and criticizing. Somehow he picked up a book by Freud, in which there was some remark to the effect that narcissistic individuals can never be cured. This Frank latched onto, and then began to view the analyses as a challenge to the analyst to beat out Freud.

After several years with the first analyst he finally did manage to relate to a woman. But then she had a breakdown. This was the end for him. The permanent triad was formed: glued in an ambivalent relationship to the analyst, he rejected every woman that came along. An unusual narcissistic grandiose defense was also formed: he said that while the analyst might know a lot, first of all he, Frank, was the most experienced patient in New York and, second, analysis had progressed only so far, so that he could no longer change, the science had not yet caught up with him. At the same time he refused to leave treatment, and when one analyst would discharge him he would simply pick up his marbles and find another. In his late sixties he leads the life of a solitary bachelor, not too miserable, but not very happy.

The case of Frank permits a reformulation of the dynamics of the interminable patient. It is the exclusion of the outside world that is the decisive factor, or, in other terms, the inability to get over the negative transference to the outside. As a regressive experience, interminability has always been connected with an excessive regression to the mother. But in terms of our present knowledge of the importance of *both* mother and father, such an explanation is insufficient. It goes back to the time when, as Freud believed, and many still do, that the earliest period of life involves for the infant nothing but attachment to an undifferentiated mass, experienced by the infant as mother. However, the infant will normally outgrow this stage of extreme dependency by moving on to the father (or the equivalent). If he does not, in terms of the triadic hypothesis, the infant has *excluded* the father, rather than over-attached itself to the mother. This provides the heuristic proposition that what should be analyzed is not so much the attachment to the analyst, as the inability to transfer to any outside object. The comfort of the analysis, or what has often been called its narcissistic gratification, can only be understood in comparison with the horror experienced in the outside world.

V
DISCUSSION

This paper offers a clarification of one essential aspect of extra-transference interpretation. This topic, as Blum (1983) points out, has been insufficiently explored. In his paper Blum writes (1983, p. 587):

> Extratransference interpretation in psychoanalysis seems to have been relegated to a psychoanalytic limbo in discussions of the theory and practice of psychoanalysis. The theory of technique has appropriately centered on the transference, and our technical precepts have not, for the most part, explicitly engaged analytic work outside the transference.

Blum goes on to consider a number of aspects of extra-transference interpretations, but attaches no specific importance or attention to the analytic triad. He does argue cogently that "a pure 'transference' position in analytic work will lead to distortions of analytic process and explanation" (Blum, 1983, p. 597).

A number of important theoretical questions arise here:

1. Is there such a thing as a non-transference relationship?
2. What is the relationship between the transference to the analyst and other transferences?
3. What are the childhood origins of the analytic triad?

1. With regard to the question of whether there are relationships that do not involve transference, Freud, in his autobiography, was quite explicit: No. "It is a universal phenomenon of the human mind." Among later authors Greenson was also quite explicit. "All object relationships consist of different admixtures and blendings of real and transference components . . . [which] should be separated from one another" (1871, p. 429).

Somehow it goes against the grain to hear that our loves for wives, sweethearts, children, friends and others are "nothing but" transferences. This is the usual resistance argument that we hear from our analysands. Yet if it offers one more narcissistic injury in a field where a series of such injuries has piled up, it still has to be faced squarely. Customarily it is blinked away or avoided, rather than faced.

Purists among psychoanalysts have tended to see the transference as a neurotic manifestation. Eissler (1953), e.g., in his famous paper on technique, stresses that ideally analysis works by interpretation alone. Strachey, in his memorable 1934 paper (later reprinted), spoke of the "mutative interpretation" as a transference interpretation, and emphasized that only such mutative interpretations could be expected to "mutate" the patient. Though he qualified his categorical statements (Blum, 1983) the influence of his paper has been strong. Yet others have disagreed with him. Thus Brenner (1976, p. 128) observed: "It seems unlikely that it is either correct or useful to take the extreme position that Strachey advocated."

Although Freud qualified his earlier statements by saying that "not every good relation between an analyst and his subject during and after analysis was to be regarded as a transference; there were also friendly relations which were based on reality and which proved to be viable'' (SE, XXIII, p. 222), the view that transference enters into all human relationships is most compatible with his entire psychology and philosophy. What he was really stressing technically was a point similar to Strachey's: that transference interpretations are the most convincing. Thus he stated: ''For a patient never forgets again what he has experienced in the form of transference; it carries a greater force of conviction than anything he can acquire in other ways'' (SE, XXIII, p. 177).

Subsequent experience indicates that this position of Freud's is exaggerated. In general, analysts will agree that transference interpretations are frequently the most cogent, but there are so many exceptions (cf. Blum, 1983, also Jacobs, 1983) that the exclusive use of transference has to be considerably modified. Stone (1961, p. 141n) explicitly took the position that ''. . . interpretations other than those directly and demonstrably impinging on the transference can be significant and effective.''

The extreme of ''transference only'' is no doubt seen in Otto Rank, whose will therapy involved so many peculiarities that it was understandably rejected by his colleagues. Others in the mainstream analytic tradition have generally taken a more modified attitude toward transference interpretation. Thus Rangell (1979, p. 84) argued that ''transference analysis, though indispensable, has also been overdone.''

Even though transference reactions are ubiquitous and universal, they have to be differentiated from the way in which the analysand learns about himself in the analysis. While in many ways transference reactions are the most useful, it seems impossible to predict with any degree of certainty just what will impress any particular patient. In fact, the careful meticulous study of the learning process in each patient is an essential part of analytic technique (Fine, 1982). Every patient learns in a different way. Even the same patient may be struck by different facets of his personality at different times. This whole problem of just what it is that induces a patient to change is one to which the analytic literature has paid too little attention.

In one case a patient almost automatically denied any interpretation that was given to him by the analyst. Then a week or two weeks later he would come in and repeat verbatim the same interpretation, with the explanation that he had been thinking about the matter and come to that conclusion on his own (Fine, 1982). Although a highly intelligent man (he was a college professor in a highly complex scientific field), he was completely oblivious of what he was doing. For the sake of the patient's progress, the analyst refrained for a long time from pointing this pattern out. When he finally did, the patient shrugged off the interpretation with the comment: "So what?" Obviously the patient, because of his early disappointments (father and mother were divorced; after he reached puberty he never set foot in his father's house), had to do it alone, and in matters that he undertook alone he usually succeeded brilliantly. The same pattern persisted in his analysis.

2. What is the relationship between the transference to the analyst and other transferences? Generalizations are impossible here but certain comments are in order.

Usually there is one significant other at a time with any analysand. The examination and comparison of the two transferences, i.e., the analytic triad, should then become the focus of the analysis. As with present and past, when the patient emphasizes the present, he has to be brought back to the past, and when he emphasizes the past he has to be brought back to the present. Thus when the patient emphasizes the transference to the analyst, he has to be brought back to the outside transference; when the patient emphasizes the outside, he has to be brought back to the transference to the analyst.

> Henry, a forty-one-year-old businessman, had a most traumatic background. Mother and father were divorced when he was five years old, after years of getting together and separating, in the course of which he was placed in two foster homes. Mother remained detached from men, never even showing any interest in one. Father later suicided. Henry had blocked off his feelings to such an extent that he could not comprehend that his mother must have been deeply hurt to withdraw from men so completely and that his father must have been deeply depressed to commit suicide.
>
> When he was twenty-five, Henry married a woman whom he adored. However, trouble soon ensued, and after some years the marriage broke up. She demanded, and received, a small amount of alimony for a few years, which imposed no burden on him; there were no children. But this proved to be the source of a strong obsession which led him to fantasize uninterruptedly that one day she would come back to him for help, and that he would refuse her.
>
> The transference to the analyst was extremely reserved. It

took him many years to admit that he had any feelings for the analyst, even though one day when he accidentally saw the analyst on the street walking in the opposite direction he hurried up to him, and put his hand on the analyst's shoulder to say hello.

The analysis for a long time centered very heavily on a comparison of the two transferences. When he longed for his ex-wife, he was angry at the analyst; when he was more positive about the analyst, he was angry at his ex-wife. It was the constant comparison that had the most effect on him therapeutically. One of the major breakthroughs came when he realized that each one served as a defense against the other.

While the functioning of the comparison of the two transferences was quite clear and convincing in the above case, it is much more obscure in many others. No doubt this is one of the major factors that accounts for the high variability among analysands, since every one has different transference figures to whom he relates, while, as with children and parents, everyone has a different feeling about the analyst.

In any case, the argument is that the awareness of the analytic triad will deepen the understanding of the transference situation, and will provide additional inroads to help the patient get better.

3. What are the childhood origins of the analytic triad? It has already been indicated that they go back to the beginnings of life. In this respect the old arguments about oral vs. Oedipal causes or interpretations become superseded. The triad is always oral and it is always Oedipal; what differentiates them is only the relative strength of the ego at each stage.

Infant research has shown that the triad is there from birth. Healthy growth involves healthy love for *both* parents. When the growth is sidetracked, which is usually the case, a conflict arises in the feelings about the parents. Then the child, in the move from mother to father, may go to father out of love for the mother (the "love affair with the world" period), or may go to father out of disappointment with the mother, or some combination of the two.

In this connection, it is worth pointing out that the role of the father in the growth process has only recently come under more careful scrutiny (Cath, Gurwitt and Ross, 1982; Lamb, 1981). As in other areas, the analytic understanding of the role of the father has stimulated investigation among the higher primates. And again, as in other fields, researchers have been surprised by what animal fathers do and can do. Redican and Taub (in Lamb, 1981, p. 223) report the following extraordinary sequence among the Barbary macaques (Macaca sylvanus):

> On four occasions, the . . . head male was the initiator of the infant's beginning to walk: he placed the animal on the ground, moving backward away from it to a distance of approximately two feet, lowering his head, looking at the infant and chattering to it. The infant would return the chatter and make crawling motions toward him . . . As the infant approached within six inches to a foot, and if no other animal except the mother was nearby, the head male would again move away and repeat the chatter. If other animals began to close in, he would pick up the infant, and move away from the crowd, making a mild gesture to them.

Apart from the early awareness of both parents and the active nature of the infant in the first year of life, two other comments come out of the theory of the analytic triad. First of all, in Mahler's rapprochement crisis, it would be more pertinent to conceptualize it as the move from mother to father, rather than the move to and away from mother. Perhaps one reason for Mahler's theoretical position is that she saw the toddlers in the experimental situation with only the mothers present; anyone who observes children at home can see quite directly how the infant wishes to move from mother to father.

Second, in the Oedipal situation, a good part of the conflict comes from the identification with the hating parent. After all, we know statistically that a large percentage of marriages break up, and among those couples who stay together, the "conflict-habituated" (Cuber and Harroff, 1965) is the type of relationship most commonly encountered. The hatred of the parents for one another has been given insufficient attention in the pathology of the child. Freud's original assumption that nothing disturbs the relationship with the parents before the Oedipal crisis was abandoned by him before the end of his career, but he never fully explored all the vicissitudes of the first year of life. The interminable patient shows that what is involved is the angry exclusion of the father and of the outside world, not just the over-attachment to mother. (This dynamic factor applies even more forcefully to the overt homosexual, whose main characteristic is the hatred of the opposite sex, not the love of his/her own sex.)

VI
SUMMARY

In the theory of transference greatest emphasis has been put on the transference to the analyst. This overlooks the transferences to other persons in the environment, which are always to be found. Generally there is one significant other person with whom the patient is involved physically. The transference to the analyst can best be understood by comparison with the transference to this other person. For this combination of two transferences I propose the term analytic triad.

Pure transference analysis, in which only the transference to the analyst is investigated, while practiced by some, has been largely dropped by mainstream analysis as too extreme. It is recognized that there are numerous extra-transference manifestations which must be analyzed as well, even though the transference to the analyst retains its great importance.

For fullest grasp and management the analytic triad must be examined as carefully as possible. A number of examples are given. The interminable patient is one who excludes the outside world, rather than one who is over-attached to the analyst.

The childhood origins of the analytic triad go back to the earliest period of life. Recent research has shown that the infant distinguishes between mother and father almost from birth on. The distinction between oral and Oedipal is one in which the strength of the ego has grown, as well as one in which the drive structure has changed. In healthy growth, the child loves both parents and develops accordingly. In pathological growth a clash between the two parents is experienced. Part of this clash derives from the identification with the hating parent.

REFERENCES

Bachrach, H. (1983). "On the Concept of Analyzability." *Psychoanalytic Quarterly,* 52: 180-204.

Balint, M. (1968). *The Basic Fault.* London: Tavistock.

Bird, B. (1972). Notes on Transference. *Journal American Psychoanalytic Association* 20: 267-301.

Bleuler, M. (1978). *The Schizophrenic Disorders.* New Haven: Yale University Press.
Blum, H.P. (1983). "The Position and Value of Extratransference Interpretation." *Journal American Psychoanalytic Association,* 31: 587-618.
Brenner, C. (1976). *Psychoanalytic Techniques and Psychic Conflict.* New York: International Universities Press.
Brome, V. (1983). *Ernest Jones: A Biography.* New York: Norton.
Cath, S.H., Gurwitt, A.R. and Ross, J.M. eds. (1982). *Father and Child.* Boston: Little and Brown.
Chiland, C. (1982). "A New Look at Fathers." *Psychoanalytic Study of the Child,* 37: 367-380.
Cuber, J. and Harroff, P. (1965). *The Significant Americans.* New York: Appleton.
Deutsch, F. (1957). A footnote to Freud's "Fragment of an Analysis of a Case of Hysteria." *Psychoanalytic Quarterly,* 26: 159-167.
Eissler, K. (1953). "The Effect of the Structure of the Ego on Psychoanalytic Technique." *Journal American Psychoanalytic Association,* 1: 104-143.
Fine, R. (1975). *Psychoanalytic Psychology.* New York: Jason Aronson.
Fine, R. (1979). *The Intimate Hour.* New York: Avery.
Fine, R. (1982). *The Healing of the Mind.* New York: Free Press - Macmillan.
Fine, R. (1984). *The Meaning of Love in Human Experience.* New York: Wiley. (In press).
Freud, S. (1905). "Fragment of an Analysis of a Case of Hysteria." *S.E.,* 7.
Freud, S. (1912). "The Dynamics of Transference." *S.E.,* 12.
Freud, S. (1920). "The Psychogenesis of a Case of Homosexuality in a Woman." *S.E.,* 18.
Freud, S. (1921). "Group Psychology and the Analysis of the Ego." *S.E.,* 18.
Freud, S. (1925). "An Autobiographical Study." *S.E.,* 20.
Freud, S. (1937). "Analysis Terminable and Interminable." *S.E.,* 23.
Gill, M. (1982). *Analysis of Transference. Vol. I.* New York: International Universities Press—Psychological Issues Monograph, 53.
Green, A. (1975). "La Psychanalyse, Son Object, Son Avenir." *Rev. Franc. Psychanalys.,* 103-134.
Greenson, R.R. (1967). *The Technique and Practice of Psychoanalysis.* New York: International Universities Press.
Greenson, R.R. (1971). "The Real Relationship Between the Patient and the Analyst." In M. Kanzer, ed. *The Unconscious Today,* 213-232. New York: International Universities Press.
Greenson, R.R. (1972). "Beyond Transference Interpretation." *International Journal Psychoanalysis,* 53: 213-217.
Greenspan, S.I. (1980). "Analysis of a Five-and-a-Half-Year-Old Girl: Implications for a Dyadic-Phallic Phase of Development." *Journal American Psychoanalytic Association,* 28: 575-603.
Greenspan, S.I. (1982). "The Second Other": The Role of the Father in Early Personality Formation and the Dyadic-Phallic Phase of Development." In S.H. Cath, A.R. Gurwitt, and J.M. Ross, eds., *Father and Child,* 123-138.
Hamburg, D. et al. (1967). "Report of Ad Hoc Committee on Central Fact-Gathering Data of the American Psychoanalytic Association." *Journal American Psychoanalytic Association,* 15: 841-861.
Herzog, J.M. (1982). "On Father Hunger: The Father's Role In the Modulation of Aggressive Drive and Fantasy." In S.H. Cath., A.R. Gurwitt, and J.M. Ross, eds. *Father and Child,* 163-174.
Jacobs, T.J. (1983). "The Analyst and the Patient's Object World: Notes on an Aspect of Countertransference." *Journal American Psychoanalytic Association,* 31: 619-642.
Jones, E. (1953-1957). *The Life and Work of Sigmund Freud.* 3 Vols. New York: Basic Books.
Kanzer, M. and Glenn, J. eds. (1980). *Freud and His Patients.* New York: Jason Aronson.
Kohut, H. (1977). *The Restoration of the Self.* New York: International Universities Press.
Lamb, M.E. (1981). *The Role of the Father in Child Development.* New York: Wiley.

Langs, R. (1976). *The Therapeutic Interaction.* 2 Vols. New York: Jason Aronson.
Lichtenberg, J.D. (1983). *Psychoanalysis and Infant Research.* Hillsdale, N.J.: Erlbaum.
Mahler, M.S. (1968). *On Human Symbiosis and the Vicissitudes of Individuation.* New York: Basic Books.
Obholzer, K. (1982). *The Wolf Man Sixty Years Later.* New York: Continuum.
Rangell, L. (1979). ''Contemporary Issues in the Theory of Therapy.'' *Journal American Psychoanalytic Association,* 27: (Supplement) 81-112.
Stolorow, R. and Lachmann, F. (1980). *Psychoanalysis of Developmental Arrests: Theory and Treatment.* New York: International Universities Press.
Strachey, J. (1934). ''The Nature of the Therapeutic Action of Psychoanalysis.'' *International Journal Psychoanalysis,* 50: 275-292.
Wolf Man (1971). *The Wolf Man.* New York: Basic Books.

Homosexuality: A Life-Style, a Civil Rights Issue or a Psycho-Social Problem?

Herbert S. Strean

Psychoanalytic, psychotherapeutic, and social work practice has always been governed by values—enduring beliefs that a specific mode of conduct or state of existence is preferable to the opposite (Rokeach, 1973). One value that has permeated the practices of mental health experts is client self-determination—the right of each person to live his or her life in a unique way, provided that it does not infringe upon the rights of others. Thus, practitioners usually do not impose their own goals or standards of behavior on their clients but concede their right to make and pursue their own decisions and plans (Hamilton, 1951; Hollis, 1964; Garrett, 1951).

As practitioners of the 1980's are confronted more and more with clients whose life-styles may differ markedly from their own—members of "gay lib," "women's lib," "one-parent families," "unmarried couples," "swingers," "switchers"—it is all the more difficult not to prejudge clients' behavior. Yet, if the therapist cannot permit the client to function in a manner that seems appropriate to him or her, diagnostic assessments will be biased, intervention plans will be disrupted, and real therapeutic help will not be forthcoming. All too often mental health has been incorrectly assumed to be the enactment of behavior that is synonymous with the tenets of the Protestant ethic—introspection, restraint, hard work, limited sexual expression (Stein and Cloward, 1958). In order for the practitioner to be an enabler and an enhancer of pleasureful and constructive living, he or she must be able to permit clients to find their own alternatives in living, even while finding these alternatives personally inimical to his or her own modus vivendi (Strean, 1978).

A corollary of the above value is another one: acceptance of each client and client-system as unique. One of the tasks of the mental health practitioner is to learn the distinctive features of each of his or her clients and client-systems. As clients (individual, family, or community) recognize from contact with their therapists that they possess skills, talents, values, and a history somewhat different from those of the rest of the world, self-esteem usually rises, optimism often grows, and clients can achieve more pleasure in living as they appreciate their own individualities.

Although most psychotherapists believe in the dignity and worth of the human being regardless of his or her social, psychological, intellectual, political orientation, sex, race, or age, it frequently takes time to resolve one's negative feelings toward individuals who hate what we love, love what we hate, value what we devalue, and devalue what we value. The practitioner, if he or she truly subscribes to a belief in the worth of every human being, must be able to empathize with the racial bigot or anti-Semite, listen attentively to the parent who abuses his or her child, offer hope to the mentally retarded and mentally ill, and see the world through the eyes of the slumlord, angry teachers, authoritarian policemen, etc. It is usually not difficult to accord dignity to clients whose beliefs are similar to our own, but it takes much self-examination and hard work to accept and identify with those individuals for whose attitudes we have customarily felt discomfort.

In appreciating, understanding, and helping clients whose life styles are different from our own, the person-situation constellation of the homosexual client—the gay man or lesbian woman—has been insufficiently clarified in practice and the literature. Many therapists who are not homosexual and who have had difficulty in feeling comfortable with the sexual practices and sexual wishes of their gay and lesbian clients have tended at times to subtly demean and castigate homosexual clients by focusing exclusively on the gay man or lesbian woman's internal dynamics and by emphasizing his or her neurotic conflicts. On the other hand, many other practitioners in their zeal to protect the right to self-determination of homosexual clients, accept their uniqueness, demonstrate their belief in the dignity, worth, and civil rights of those clients, and have contended that practitioners who make diagnostic assessments of homosexual clients, particularly of their sexual conflicts, are acting out biases and discriminating against them (Bonnefil, 1982).

In trying to achieve a balanced perspective in clinical work with gay or lesbian clients, it is imperative for the practitioner to understand and differentiate between the client's life style, his or her civil rights, and his or her idiosyncratic psychodynamics which interact with his or her unique situation.

SOCIOLOGICAL CONSIDERATIONS

Regardless of their own sexual preferences, theoretical predilections, or favored therapeutic modalities, all practitioners must recognize that from a societal perspective, homosexuality is a socially deviant form of behavior (Weinberg and Williams, 1974; Hite, 1976). By social deviancy, we are referring to any form of behavior which the broader culture or subculture has alleged to be either unacceptable, improper, or illegal (Becker, 1973; Merton, 1957; Parsons, 1951).

The subjective nature of the label, "social deviant," becomes apparent when a significant group in the culture at a given time labels as aberrant, behavior which it considers appropriate at another time. Murder, for example, is deemed to be quite unacceptable by most politicians and they have taken many steps for countless decades to prevent its occurrence in most social sectors. However, these same politicians have also passed numerous bills sanctioning murder. This was poignantly demonstrated during the Vietnam War, when the President of the United States and Congress were sanctioning murder in Asia but concomitantly declaring another war to exterminate manslaughter and other forms of crime in the streets. Although many jurists and other leaders in government will ardently condemn the notion of killing another human being, these same individuals have recommended that the best form of punishment for killing is to kill the killer! Furthermore, many individuals who are against abortion because they believe it is a form of murder are very much for capital punishment.

Not only may the same group label the same behavior "deviant" at one time and "healthy" or "appropriate" at another, depending on the behavior's social context, but different social groups take different stances on identical behavior. For example, the behavior of Joan of Arc was defined as not only appropriate in her day, but she was considered to be a heroine and hailed as a truly remarkable lady. The same behavior exhibited in most places in the world today would be labeled as paranoid schizophrenia, because Joan of Arc heard voices telling her to save her country.

Although an adult brutally hurting a child is often considered, in a social and in a legal sense, as child abuse, Abraham in the Holy Bible is revered to this day as someone who was very pious and far from a criminal for wanting to murder his son, Isaac, and sacrifice him to God.

The notion that "social deviancy" is an arbitrary, subjective label is best illustrated in the way homosexuality has been viewed by significant social groups over the years. Championed in Ancient Greece, rewarded in Caesar's Rome, but repudiated in Victorian England, homosexuality has been received most ambivalently in the United States. Homosexuals have been punished severely by the United States Army and other institutions for several decades and homosexuality has been considered a disease by many medically oriented therapists. Yet homosexuality has been upheld by the Gay Liberation, and fairly recently it was stricken as a classification of illness from the psychiatric nomenclature of the American Psychiatric Association. Although many groups in American society have questioned whether homosexual men or women can be mature foster parents, New York State has now legally sanctioned homosexuals to be foster parents and this move has received wide support from many professional and nonprofessional sectors of society (*New York Times,* August 27, 1982).

Homosexuality and the Audience

From a sociological perspective, it would appear that homosexuality, like other behaviors that are labeled socially deviant, is best understood not so much from the quality of the act, but from the interaction between a person who commits the act and those who respond to it (Erikson, 1957; Becker, 1963).

As Kai Erikson has stated:

> Deviance is not a property inherent in certain forms of behavior, it is a property conferred upon those forms by the audiences which directly or indirectly witness them. The critical variable in the study of deviance, then, is the social audience rather than the individual actor, since it is the audience which

> eventually determines whether or not any episode of behavior or any class of episodes is labeled deviant. (Erikson, 1957, p. 11)

Similarly, the sociologist Becker has opined: "Social groups create deviance by making rules whose infractions constitute deviance and by applying those rules to particular people and labeling them as outsiders" (Becker, 1963, p. 9).

When an audience labels a form of behavior such as homosexuality as deviant, the deviant behavior is utilized by society to buttress its value and norms (Goffman, 1961; Lemert, 1951) and in every society there are dominant values and norms which key groups in it wish to maintain. Consequently, one way of preserving honesty is to locate those who are dishonest and punish them; one means of sustaining the marital institution is by disapproving of adultery; and by referring truants to child guidance clinics and juvenile courts, society reaffirms the importance it places on children attending school (Merton, 1951). Homosexuality, therefore, cannot be simply dismissed as behavior which disrupts society—a stance taken by the Moral Majority and other social action and religious groups—but is frequently repudiated because it is society's major means of championing heterosexuality when heterosexuality is its dominant norm and value.

Once a homosexual or any other person has been labeled as socially deviant, he has enormous difficulty modifying how others view him. In the eyes of the dominant society, he has failed in living and must give allegiance to an anomalous conception of himself and the world (Gove, 1970; Becker, 1963; Lemert, 1951).

Social Deviancy, Civil Rights, and Mental Health

If we accept the premise that "social deviancy" is in many ways arbitrarily defined, varies from social context to social context, and is essentially a subjective notion, our next step is to evaluate the position of the helping professional vis à vis the norm setters of society. Those who have researched the subject (Lennard and Bernstein, 1969; Kahn, 1973; Reissman, Cohen and Pearl, 1964; Davis, 1958; Hollingshead and Redlich, 1958) almost unanimously conclude that those who are in the mental health professions tend to equate "mental health" with the dominant norms of society. As Davis (1958) has pointed out, many of the persistent refrains emanating from mental hygienists are quite consistent with the Protestant ethic—work, discipline, heterosexual marriage.

Because the mental health movement contributes to the maintenance and persistence of the middle-class sociocultural structure by providing authoritative "scientific" support to traditional values, it should not come as a surprise that there is a peculiar collusion between many mental hygienists and the major upholders of middle-class norms. This collusion is particularly apparent in the violation of civil rights of gay men and lesbian women.

There have been numerous newspaper accounts showing that when teachers, members of the military, politicians, and others are suspected of being homosexual, they are frequently turned over to a mental hygiene professional who is asked to determine how much of a danger these people are to their charges. If they refuse to be examined, they are often threatened with job loss, and if they consent to be examined they are frequently diagnosed as "emotionally disturbed." What is so often overlooked in determining the fate of homosexual employees is their job abilities, skills, and knowledge. Their alleged "psychiatric disturbance" is usually decisive.

It is of interest that when men or women teachers who are homosexual are "discovered," one of the ever-present fears of parents and administrative officials is that they will sexually seduce children of their same gender. It is very rarely presumed, yet it has occurred, that a heterosexual teacher will seduce students of the opposite sex.

As we will demonstrate later, homosexual men and women, like most people—all of us and all of our clients—have some maturational lags and emotional conflicts. However, as clinicians can avow, there is no direct correlation between maturational conflicts and poor job performance. Furthermore, mental health professionals have recognized that there is a huge range of possible behavior within one given psychiatric category, whether the category be neurotic, psychotic, borderline, or sexually deviant. If a person does choose members of his or her own sex as exclusive sexual partners, this person may be aggressive or passive, very egocentric or quite altruistic, impulsive or controlled, intelligent or unintelligent.

Because labels like "deviant," "sexual dysfunction," "perversion," or "antisocial character" do not fully describe an individual but tend to categorize and to stereotype him or her, they offer little predictive power in fully determining psychosocial functioning (Fine, 1982; Fine, 1981; Strean, 1979). Furthermore, many forms of behavior which are considered socially deviant such as homosexuality may be *less* psychologically debilitating than emotional problems that are tolerated by society. For example, religious zeal may be a manifestation of severe neurotic conflicts but rare is the zealot who is referred for psychiatric consultation because his religious preoccupations might interfere with his job performance.

It becomes apparent that when the clinician wants to honor the homosexual client's civil rights, to protect his or her freedom of self-determination, and to guarantee his or her dignity and self-worth, the practitioner must not be an administrative or legal officer who determines whether the person works, lives or plays in a specified social context. Rather, the clinician's job is to help those individuals who want help with the interpersonal, their social, their psychological and sometimes with their sexual problems.

CLINICAL ISSUES

Recognizing that the homosexual client has been arbitrarily labelled as "deviant" and that deviancy varies from social context to social context, and is further modified by historical, military, political, and other social and economic factors, we are now in a position to discuss the clinician's role in working with the homosexual client in treatment.

In trying to help a homosexual man or woman therapeutically, the objective, empathetic, and mature clinician, as with any client, accepts the homosexual client where he or she is (Hamilton, 1951; Hollis, 1964; Perlman, 1957). Many homosexual clients seek a therapist, not because they are suffering from interpersonal, situational, or psychic pains which, in their minds at least, are not directly related to their sexual preferences. It is crucial when involving these homosexual clients in treatment, that their own concerns be given top priority; otherwise they can feel misunderstood and leave treatment.

> Miss A., a twenty-six-year-old woman, sought therapeutic help because she was in a depression. She was dissatisfied with her work, hated living alone, and felt very "unlovable" in most interpersonal situations. To cope with her strong depression, she was using alcohol and drugs and was worried about becoming an addict. In addition, Miss A. reported that she was suffering from nightmares which frightened her so much that she spent many hours awake each night.

> Miss A. responded very positively to her female therapist's interest and concern. In her third interview, Miss A. said to her therapist, "I like the idea of having a friendly listener who does not impose her own ideas on me. You know, I've been sleeping a little better and feeling less depressed."
>
> Feeling accepted by her therapist, Miss A., in her sixth interview, confided that she was a lesbian but had not been able to find a sexual partner in several months. Here the therapist stopped being a quiet, attentive and accepting listener and began, instead, to make several comments. The therapist said that it was probably more difficult for Miss A. to have a sexual partner than it was for most people, because Miss A. was "a member of a minority." She also started to ask Miss A. several questions about the etiology of her sexual preferences.
>
> Although Miss A. seemed to cooperate with her therapist in her last interview, she did not return for further appointments, saying over the phone that she had "found a way to take care of myself."

In the above vignette, the therapist was obviously uncomfortable hearing about her client's homosexuality and handled her discomfort by becoming over-active, over-supportive, and intrusive. Feeling misunderstood, the client had to "take care of myself."

When clinicians have not resolved their own attitudes about homosexuality and have not come to grips with their homosexual fantasies, wishes, or experiences, they can behave quite anxiously with their homosexual clients and become too reassuring, too supportive, or too active, or, they can do the opposite and become critical, rejecting or withdrawn.

When the practitioner moves away from reflective listening and does not take sufficient time to hear the homosexual client's past and present life story so that ego functions, psychosexual development, and inner and outer conflicts can be assessed well, he or she is probably having difficulty coping with his or her own anxiety about homosexuality. One means of coping with the anxiety that a client's homosexuality induces in the practitioner is to tell the client that homosexuality is a legitimate way of life that should never be condemned.

> Mr. B., age thirty, was in treatment with a male therapist. At the client's fourth appointment he told his therapist that he

> was "gay." The therapist did not wait for Mr. B. to talk further about his being gay and how he, Mr. B., felt about it, but stated, "You are a human being like everybody else and should not feel ashamed of your sexuality."
>
> Mr. B. went on to say that he knew he "was different," that perhaps his "homosexuality was caused by a neurosis" and that maybe the therapist was "going overboard to be kind." The more Mr. B. questioned his homosexuality, the more the therapist reassured him. Consequently, Mr. B. felt misunderstood and left treatment prematurely.

Every member of a minority has to cope with feelings of being different from the majority (Stein and Cloward, 1958; Reissman, Cohen and Pearl, 1964). Although Jews have referred to themselves as God's Chosen People and Blacks have described themselves as beautiful, the therapist cannot assume, ipso facto, that the homosexual is always "gay" in the sense that he or she is always happy.

The homosexual client may have latent doubts about his or her sexual orientation and these doubts, when they emerge in the treatment encounter, need to be ventilated and explored. As we saw in the case of Mr. B., when he was very much reassured by his therapist, he became suspicious and left treatment.

If practitioners truly accept their homosexual clients as they are and relate to their genuine concerns, some homosexual clients begin to feel more strengthened in their sexual predilections while others begin to examine the dynamic reasons for their sexual inclinations. As the client moves with more certainty toward a sexual alternative, the therapist must be very aware of his or her own biases, lest he or she does not impose them on the client. This is similar to situations where the practitioner can subtly champion a particular alternative that he or she believes the client should choose, such as a job or a career change, a divorce, a marriage, etc. Rather than help the client determine what he or she wants to do, the clinician steers the client in the direction of his or her own biases.

When the therapist listens, but does not judge, empathizes, but does not direct, the homosexual client like all clients, feels safer to be himself or herself and the treatment can become an intensive and constructive experience in exploring one's self.

> Mr. C., a thirty-three-year-old man, who practiced homosexuality exclusively, sought treatment for depression, loneliness, and many psychosomatic complaints. He became emo-

tionally involved with the therapist quite early in his treatment because he "liked the idea of just talking about whatever comes to my mind." The ventilation of aggression toward his parents, complaints about his male therapist for not loving him enough, and "the attention I get from you sometimes," reduced his sense of loneliness, depression, and psychosomatic complaints after a few months of twice-a-week therapy.

When the client's wishes to have a homosexual affair with the therapist became the focus of treatment, and the therapist explored the client's fantasies toward him (rather than gratifying them) the client told the therapist that he abhorred him, similar to the way he abhorred both of his parents. The therapist, like Mr. C.'s parents, never fondled him, fed him, or "tickled" him and this proved to Mr. C. that they hated him.

With the release of bottled-up aggression, Mr. C.'s ego functions began to emerge in a more mature fashion. He became less demanding, less angry, and could enjoy pleasure more. After a year of treatment, referring to his homosexuality, Mr. C. remarked to his therapist, "Isn't it crazy to want to punish my parents by going against the tide?" For Mr. C., his homosexuality was in part an expression of opposition toward his parents.

As Mr. C. psychologically gained some separation from his introjected parents, he began to feel less afraid of his normal aggression and assertiveness. As he needed to be less of an angry child and developed more autonomy and maturity as a person, he started to consider what frightened him about participating in heterosexual relationships.

It should be noted in the above example that Mr. C.'s concerns were given top priority by the therapist and the client felt freer to explore himself. First, he shared his murderous fantasies with the therapist and then later he made the therapist an object of his sexual fantasies. When the therapist is made an object of the homosexual client's sexual fantasies, it is important, of course, for the therapist to be accepting without being seductive, and understanding without being detached.

The case of Mr. C. also raises the question about some of the dynamics that have been unravelled in clinical research on homosexuality. What findings do clinical research on homosexuality yield?

Clinical Research on Homosexuality

One of the consistent findings of clinical research is that all human beings have unconscious desires to be a member of the opposite sex (Freud, 1938; Wyss, 1973; Karasu and Socarides, 1979). Most clinicians who have been engaged in intensive therapy have noted that boys and men have wishes to have breasts and babies, and girls and women often fantasy that the life of a male would be better. Perhaps in our competitive culture, the grass often seems greener on the other side.

Clinical researchers have also found that those who repudiate homosexuality the most, are often trying to deny their own homosexual fantasies (Fine, 1982; Fenichel, 1945). The late Senator Joseph McCarthy was an outstanding and punitive opponent of homosexual rights, yet it was also alleged that he found his own intense homosexual desires intolerable. For those of us who have been therapists in institutions like the army or prisons, where homosexual urges are often stimulated, we have discovered that the administrative personnel of these facilities are often most condemning of homosexual practices. It is now a virtual truism in dynamic psychotherapy that individuals repudiate in others what they cannot tolerate in themselves (English and Pearson, 1945).

Another of the findings from clinical research is that exclusive homosexuality is rarely found among people who have had consistently gratifying love experiences with their parents (Socarides, 1978; Rieber, 1962; Fine, 1981). Homosexual clients often do attest to the fact that a total denial of the opposite sex can come out of a background of severe childhood frustration. Often, when a homosexual pair is examined closely, the observer sees an enormous amount of vulnerability, uncertainty and revenge in both partners. In many cases, the two are acting out a fantasied mother-child relationship (Socarides, 1978).

In combining clinical research on homosexuality with the sociological research that we have reviewed earlier, the clinician's perspective on the subject is very much enriched. From a sociological perspective we have seen how society labels homosexuals as deviants and punishes them, often denies them their civil rights, and tries to get mental health professionals and others to participate in censuring them. This societal position does a tremendous disservice to these clients and compounds problems for people who usually have had unfulfilling interpersonal relationships in childhood.

Homosexual clients need therapeutic understanding, not censure. They need to talk about their lives, not have their lifestyles condemned.

Although many clinicians have demonstrated the profound psychic pain and conflict in homosexual clients, their results have been questioned because they have supposedly worked from a skewed sample—clients in treatment. While it is true that people in treatment are usually *more* mature than those who do not have the courage to confront themselves and face their immaturities and irrationalities, the similarities between the two groups are probably much greater than the differences. As Harry Stack Sullivan once said, "We are all more human than otherwise."

Many lay and professional groups tend to assume that if a person is in distress about his or her conflicts and seeks out therapy, this is less mature than the individual who wishes to ignore psychic conflicts. Distress about a problem may be viewed as healthier than lack of distress and it is quite possible that some of the homosexual men and women who repudiate their need for psychotherapy may be using repression and/or denial (Fine, 1981).

In working with the problems of homosexual clients psychotherapists in all disciplines have many responsibilities. They have to respect and accept a life-style that is frequently different from their own, behave in a way that at all times guarantees the homosexual client's civil rights, and maintain an objective eye and an empathetic ear as they work with clients who have frequently been scapegoated as children by their parents and discriminated as adults by an intolerant society.

REFERENCES

Becker, H., 1963. *Outsiders: Studies in the Sociology of Deviance.* New York: The Free Press.

Bieber, I., 1962. *Homosexuality.* New York: Basic Books.

Bonnefil, M., 1982. Discussant of "A Critique of the New Treatment Modalities," in *Controversy in Psychotherapy,* ed. H. Strean, Metuchen, New Jersey, Scarecrow Press.

Davis, K., 1958. "Mental Hygiene and the Class Structure," in *Social Perspectives on Behavior,* eds. H. Stein and R. Cloward, New York: The Free Press.

English, O. and G. Pearson, 1945. *Emotional Problems of Living.* New York: W.W. Norton.

Erikson, K., 1964. "Notes on the Sociology of Deviance," in *The Other Side,* ed. H. Becker, New York: The Free Press.

Fenichel, O., 1945. *The Psychoanalytic Theory of Neuroses.* New York: W.W. Norton.

Fine, R., 1982. *The Healing of the Mind,* 2nd Edition, New York: The Free Press.

Fine, R., 1981. *The Psychoanalytic Vision.* New York: The Free Press.

Freud, S., 1938. *The Basic Writings of Sigmund Freud.* New York: Random House, The Modern Library.
Garrett, A., 1951. *Interviewing: Its Principles and Methods.* New York: Family Service Association of America.
Goffman, E., 1961. *Asylums.* Garden City, New York: Anchor Books.
Gove, W., 1970. "Societal Reaction as an Explanation of Mental Illness: An Evaluation," *American Sociological Review,* Vol. 35, No. 5, pp. 873-883.
Hamilton, G., 1951. *The Theory and Practice of Social Casework.* New York: Columbia University Press.
Hite, S., 1976. *The Hite Report.* New York: Macmillan.
Hollingshead, A. and F. Redlich, 1958. "Social Stratification and Psychiatric Disorders," in *Social Perspectives on Behavior,* eds. H. Stein and R. Cloward, New York: The Free Press.
Hollis, F., 1964. *Casework: A Psychosocial Therapy.* New York: Random House.
Kahn, A., 1973. *Shaping the New Social Work.* New York: Columbia University Press.
Karasu, T. and C. Socarides, 1979. *On Sexuality.* New York: International University Press.
Lemert, E., 1951. *Social Pathology.* New York: McGraw-Hill.
Lennard H. and A. Bernstein, 1969. *Patterns in Human Interaction.* San Francisco: Jossey-Bass.
Merton, R., 1957. *Social Theory and Social Structure.* Glencoe, Illinois, The Free Press.
New York Times, August 27, 1982.
Parsons, T., 1951. *The Social System.* Glencoe, Illinois: The Free Press.
Perlman, H., 1957. *Social Casework: A Problem Solving Process.* Chicago: University of Chicago Press.
Riessman, F., J. Cohen, and A. Pearl, 1964. *Mental Health of the Poor.* New York: The Free Press.
Rokeach, M., 1973. *The Nature of Human Values.* New York: The Free Press.
Socarides, C., 1978. *Homosexuality.* New York: Jason Aronson.
Stein, H. and R. Cloward, 1958. *Social Perspectives on Behavior.* New York: The Free Press.
Strean, H., 1979. *Psychoanalytic Theory and Social Work Practice.* New York: The Free Press.
Strean, H., 1979. *Clinical Social Work.* New York: The Free Press.
Weinberg, M. and C. Williams, 1974. *Male Homosexuals.* New York: Oxford University Press.
Wyss, D., 1973. *Psychoanalytic Schools.* New York: Jason Aronson.

Negative Voyeurism and Its Application to Psychoanalytic Practice

Robert C. Lane

ORIENTATION AND VIEW

Freud (13) points out that the aim of the scoptophilic instinct is to watch during the voiding of urine and feces, and after this tendency has been repressed, to look at the genitals of others, both one's own sex and those of the opposite sex. Freud, in "Three Essays on the Theory of Sexuality," did not discuss the wish to look at the breast or to watch others nurse, which in time precedes the above wishes. Yet, he did say in 1905 (13):

> He who sees a satiated child sink back from the mother's breast and fall asleep with reddened cheeks and blissful smile, will have to admit that this picture remains as typical of the expression of sexual gratification in later life.

Scoptophilia (looking) was described by Freud as a partial or component instinct along with showing off and cruelty. However, he later changed in his attitude towards the partial or component instincts. In 1905 (13), he pointed out that the infantile sexual life ". . . though mainly under the control of erogenous zones, also shows components which from the very beginning point to other persons as sexual objects." These were initially said ". . . to manifest themselves independently of the erogenous zones, and only later enter into intimate relation with the sexual life." Freud also said in this paper (13), ". . . from the bodily organs two kinds of excitation arise which are founded upon differences of a chemical na-

The author would like to express his appreciation to Judith Felton, Ph.D., for her very perceptive comments and suggestions, all of which have been integrated into the text. She made the author realize how much there is still to be learned and how easy it is to miss the obvious.

ture. One of these forms of overstimulation can be designated as specifically sexual, and the concerned organ as an erogenous zone, while the sexual element emanating from it is a partial impulse."

In his paper "On Narcissism" in 1914 (18), Freud placed the reservoir of libido in the ego, which raised questions regarding the whole relationship between libido and ego and challenged the libido theory. In 1915 (19), he found himself in difficulty trying to maintain his original position in reference to the component instincts. In his "Instincts and their Vicissitudes" (19), he could not fit love and hate into the "scheme of instincts," and concluded that the origin of hate is not derived from the sexual life but from the ego's struggle for preservation. Thus, he was postulating a more primary sadistic drive that was apart from libidinal wishes, on which he elaborated in 1920 (20). Reuben Fine, in his book *Freud, A Critical Re-Evaluation of his Theories* (11), summarizes the revisions in the libido theory. In the paper on the vicissitudes of instincts, Freud described and delineated the relationship between sexual gazing (scoptophilia) and self-display and called these instincts voyeurism and exhibitionism. At this time, he pointed out that scoptophilia at the onset of its activity is auto-erotic, " . . . it has indeed an object, but that object is the subject's own body," and only later shifts "by the way of comparison" from the self to others. Freud had first said that the component instincts involve other people as objects. In the 1915 paper (19), he said that the subject looks at his own sexual organ or his own sexual organ is looked at by himself, then the subject looks at an extraneous object (scoptophilia-active), and his own sexual organ is looked at by another person (exhibitionism-passive): "One changed into the other by a reversal from active to passive and by a turning round on the subject." The preliminary phase of the scoptophilic instinct, when the subject's own body is the object of the scoptophilia (auto-erotic satisfaction), is a narcissistic stage.

In summary, Freud's view was that the partial instinct of scoptophilia, the main component in children's sexual curiosity (14), is constant, manifesting itself over and over again, and is present in all of us in the form of looking, investigating, exploring, curiosity, inquisitiveness, and the wish to know. It is made up of different parts of other instincts and is attached to these other instincts (components of them). We do not know the source of the instinct but the aim is to gain sexual gratification by looking, and the object is initially auto-erotic and narcissistic and then shifts to objects when we are able to compare ourselves with others. Scoptophilia is one of the major initiators of excitement in sex play in the form of forepleasure and if it is too strong or too repressed it may replace genital primacy as the main source of gratification. Freud pointed out (13) that looking becomes a perversion "(a) when it is exclusively limited to the genitals; (b) when it becomes connected with the overcoming or loathing (voyeurs and onlookers at the function of excretion); and (c) when instead of preparing for the normal sexual aim, it suppresses it."

Freud felt the instincts were biologically determined, and wrote about them in terms of the libidinal forces present at the various age levels. The more recent psychoanalytic methodology (4,33,34,38, 40,41) stresses the characterization of the early parent-child relationship and the unconscious fantasies and problems of all family members. The contemporary view places a much stronger emphasis on developmental factors: the importance of the mother touching, holding, grasping, rocking and looking at the child in the early weeks of life. The child in the second month begins to notice his world as perceptual apparatus develops, and now can look back at the mother. The relationship between the baby's body (subject, self, inner) and the environment (object, mother, outer) must be reviewed in terms of their interaction.

There may be strong visual cathexis from the earliest days of an infant's life. Pleasure in looking and the early sexualization of sight is intimately connected with the mother-child relationship. The mother (or mother surrogate) brings all her voyeuristic-exhibitionistic conflicts and prior experiences into the mother-child relationship. She must look at the child and the child must look at her, looking being an integral part of all object relations. How, when, in what way, at what and how often the mother looks and the messages conveyed to the child by her looking (sensuality, sexuality, hostility, rejection, tenderness, warmth) play a very important role in the development of the child's voyeurism and in his general sense of identification. The mother's healthy ability to handle (neutralize) her scoptophilic tendencies helps the child to handle his. What or who the child represents to her (penis, feces, father, mother, brother or sister), is dependent on her own fixations both on the levels of psychosexual development and object relationships. The structural conflicts of the mother are forever influencing the child's behavior and development of his sense of self (5). The greater the ambivalence to the child, the greater the conflict in looking at the child.

Voyeurism may attach itself to each of the psychosexual stages or the erogenous zones attached to them. On an oral level, there may be a strong impulse to look at breasts, or children being nursed; the larger the breast, the more the milk in fantasy, and the greater the curiosity and desire to look. The child knows that hunger will be appeased when he sees the mother's breast, and the infant who desires it, hallucinates it (all of Lewin's work on the dream screen [30,31,32] is relevant here). Oral voyeurism may reveal itself in an overwhelming envy of those who are fed or enjoy their food. A constant looking at another person's plate to see how much he is getting or an insatiable greed are further examples: the breast or bottle is equated with food and love.

Fenichel (9) speaks of displacement of hunger to the mental field and to reading, taking in knowledge and learning in particular. Lane and Storch (28) discuss this point in a previous article. The wish to know sexual facts can substitute for, or be a displacement of, the wish to look at sexual facts and becomes a sexual aim in itself. This may lead to the asking of many questions, the search for book knowledge, or the wish to listen to sexual material. We might call this activity "aural voyeurism." Fenichel (9), as well as others, saw reading as an oral voyeuristic trait (looking equals eating, reading as a substitute for eating): " . . . voracious looking can be recognized as a substitute for gluttony." This view was held by Strachey (39), Jarvis (24) and others, while the taking in of knowledge as an oral voyeuristic trait was discussed by Lewin (29), Emch (7), Lane and Storch (28) and others.

Curiosity for knowledge, according to Fenichel, may become an oral character trait and " . . . under certain conditions assume all the voracity of the original oral appetite" (9). When reading matter or material is sexualized or a search for pornographic passages occurs (pornography has anal implications as well), or reading is used like viewing a pornographic film to cause excitement, resulting in masturbation or other sexual activities, a reading block may occur. Freud (16) said, "The histories of obsessional patients almost invariably reveal an early development and premature repression of the sexual instinct of looking and knowing (the scoptophilic and epistomophilic instincts)." He also said in this paper, " . . . the very high average intellectual capacity among obsessional patients is probably also connected with this fact." Reading is usually not pathological but a healthy sublimation of the scoptophilic instinct.

It has in the past been quite fashionable to expose all but the nipple of the breast and many magazines have played into the oral voyeuristic needs of readers (lookers). The name of a magazine (*Look, See, Glare, Stare, Peep, Glance* and the like), as well as its content, attempted to appeal to voyeuristic interests. The search for the hourglass figure with a breast-buttock emphasis (buttocks equal breasts) often is a form of oral voyeurism. Today this appears to be less common among younger men, who prefer slimmer and more athletic women. Although, historically, men have been described as being more orally voyeuristic than women (gender difference), women are becoming increasingly "orally voyeuristic" and similar to men. More than in the past, they notice and verbalize their search for the broad-shouldered, slim-waisted male with a large penis. One example is the increased attendance of women at male strip shows (sticking dollar bills down their briefs). This is also a form of anal voyeurism, similar to the pathology described in relation to men.

Not only may that which is looked at have oral, anal or phallic significance, but the eye itself may be an important symbol. The eye was recognized by Freud (12,13,17) and Abraham (1) to be both a phallic and oral incorporative symbol. Many authors felt that to be blinded equalled to be castrated. The eye may also be a symbol of the breast and uterus/vagina combination as well. Ophthalmological surgeons have described the removal of a cataract, which is "delivered" from the eye, as similar to the delivery of a baby. In addition, the eye in its external shape and form, with a central pupil is similar to the breast and nipple. Finally, its internal structure, is also able to be associated with the breast as easily as with the vagina. Some authorities suggest the eye is basic to brain and body functions and has primal implications, more breastlike (primal) than genital.

Both Abraham (1) and Fenichel (8) spoke of the bisexual function of the eye. Fenichel (8) described the glaring evil eye of the basilisk, snake, hypnotist and witch, all of which, he felt, caused paralysis, immobility and stiffness (turning into stone). To Fenichel, they were symbols of the female genital organ as was the Head of Medusa (10,21). He pointed out that in the unconscious all kinds of contradictions occur, thus turning stiff or to stone means both having an erection and death or castration. For a more complete study of the use of the eye as a symbol and symptom, see Hart (23).

Voyeurism itself is an act of incorporation, taking in with the eye is an extension of orality. Fenichel (8) says:

> Every pregenital component of the sexual instinct is part auto-

> erotic and in part directed towards objects. In so far as pregenital instinctual impulses are directed towards objects, their object relations are primitive and the primitive object relations, the precursor of love and hate, is incorporation.

Abraham (2) shared the above view. Fenichel (8) indicated that in the unconscious to look at an object may suggest the wish to devour or incorporate it, to destroy or injure it, or to assure oneself that the object is not yet injured or destroyed. To Fenichel, to look at an object also suggested the wish to share or participate by means of empathy in its experience, such as to grow like the object or conversely to force it to grow like oneself.

He (8) made the point that " . . . the wish to incorporate what I see and to participate in the experience of that which I see are identical." He emphasized the use of the eye as a castrating sadistic organ. The looker may wish to see the insides of the body, which he may picture as a place of bloodshed where one is devoured. Or looking may represent the destruction and oral introjection of the pregnant body or the penis. The wish to see the penis or insides of the body and to destroy them, and the wish to be the penis or child become one and the same via identification, according to Fenichel. "I want to look at the penis, to see it; I want to hurt or destroy the penis, I want to castrate someone; I want to see if someone is castrated, to see how they are castrated; I want a penis, I want to be the penis; and I want to be castrated," are all related wishes of the scoptophilic ("I wish to look, to tear it out or push it in, to eat it up, to put myself in its place, to grow like it, to take it over, to become it").

Voyeurism can have an anal function, an interest and pleasure in one's own excrement and its derivatives or in the productions of others. Extreme envy of the productions of others and constant searching and looking to see what others make, do or leave behind, are forms of anal voyeurism. Related to anal voyeurism is the idea that voyeurism can have a negative quality, rejecting the product or object, considering it to be evil. Although known to all therapists, there is nothing specific in the literature on this.

One form of anal exhibitionism is "mooning." This peculiar practice, to the best of my knowledge, was not publicized prior to the sixties. Mooning is dropping the pants and showing one's backside. Little children often will exhibit their rumps, giggle and act coy and seductive while the adults around them look at and pinch the children's backsides. Mooning may well reflect a problem of our times. Boys were mooning while riding in cars, sticking their backsides out of the windows. Some years ago, I treated a boy whose best friend was expelled from college for mooning a girl. Another patient, a college student, told me he mooned the "First Lady" from a hotel window as she was passing by car in the street below.

The meaning of this type of exhibitionism needs further discussion. To show one's backside may suggest scorn, contempt, a wish to startle, and a wish to shame and humiliate by revealing that part of the body from which one defecates. It may also be a symptom of preoedipal issues or developmental arrests. It can reflect a "looking to" the voyeur for a mirroring, validating, or admiring response. It was believed by many analysts that the buttocks are the feminine rather than the masculine side of man, in that they are common to both sexes. Other analysts feel that the buttocks are neither feminine nor masculine. Although it is logical that a female with anxiety about femininity (phobic or with penis envy) or a male with anxiety about masculinity (castration anxiety or with penis envy) would be more likely to interpret the buttocks as representational of one gender or the other. Fenichel (8) felt that the moon stood for an eye and by looking at it, one identified with it. Thus, to moon or exhibit the buttocks possibly suggests the wish to look at them.

The phallic quality of voyeurism, the wish to look at genitals, is the most common form. It should be mentioned that the most frequent form of voyeurism seen in our courts concerns the "Peeping Tom" or voyeur. These individuals frequent certain neighborhoods, hiding in the bushes or on rooftops with the purpose of waiting in excitement for women to undress and then watching them. The voyeurs hope to witness in addition some sexual act, such as masturbation or intercourse. They use the eye to excite and stimulate and usually masturbate while watching. Certain of these voyeurs pick their sites, with a different locality for different days. Others are floaters or cruisers, going here and there to see what they can see. I had a patient who, during the war years, would travel from his camp to New York, a considerable distance, spend time on rooftops, and return to base in time to make reveille. Many of these voyeurs have very seductive mothers and their activity often is a repetition of an earlier witnessed experience in the hope of mastering anxiety and excitement. Other males may need to look at female genitals as a hostile act toward women whom they fear. This male hostility toward women who are feared is more of a problem in our times—and before—than the mooning one. One may ask why do not girls with seductive fathers become "Peeping Tomasinas?" This raises the issue of gender differences in the development of this type of pathology. Although more is needed to explain the psychodynamics of the sexual difference, women are inclined to repress their voyeuristic impulses, in part because they tend, more than men, to fear their aggressive and hostile wishes.

Myers (35), as well as Freud (13) and Fenichel (9), points out that repeated exposure to the primal scene may traumatize the patient. He also feels primal scene exposure leads to learning problems and a compulsion for patients to repeat the experience with their own children. The voyeur tries to repeat the scene in an attempt to master it and deny what he saw. As no sight can bring about complete reassurance, voyeurs have to look again and again and attempt to see more and more. The voyeur's insatiability can lead to greater and greater sadomasochistic behavior. The child may identify with either partner in the primal scene, but more often identifies with the adult of the opposite sex. Helpless yet fascinated in the face of strong excitation, terrified of castration, the child identifies with what was seen and both wishes and is tempted to repeat the experience.

Many patients who report having witnessed the primal scene as children speak of their extreme feeling of loneliness, being ignored, not wanted or needed or a part of their parents (3). The voyeur is experiencing a vicarious act which suggests an inhibition of the desire to touch an object. The voyeur is on the outside looking in and would like to be on the inside, part of, sharing, participating, initiating. Each instinct seems to have its own affect and the affect most associated with scoptophilia (other than the guilt it engenders) appears to be loneliness.

DEFINITION OF NEGATIVE VOYEURISM

Negative voyeurism as applied in this paper refers to the wish to look at another person and to find something negative or wrong with him/her (to reject the product or object and consider it evil). It may take the form of criticism, fault-finding, nagging, harping, carping, looking for a deficiency or imperfection, or something missing or lacking. It may be focused on something a person does or does not do. It usually results in a feeling of being picked on or apart, taken advantage of, used, ridiculed, intimidated and humiliated. It reflects a feeling of castration in the negative voyeur, and is associated with dissatisfaction, inadequacy, disappointment, deficiency, or unhappiness which is projected and may result in anger in some form, the extreme of which is hatred and a feeling of persecution.

In Freudian language, negative voyeurism refers to a fixation on the anal level, a wish to look at the back side of the object rather than the front side, the negative side rather than the positive side, the bad side rather than the good side; a wish to find nothing rather than something, a concern with the dead rather than the living, the anal rather than the genital. Fromm (22) calls these people necrophiles as opposed to biophiles. Negative voyeurs thus look for evil (feces and defecation) everywhere and its many derivatives (things or forms that may symbolize evil: death, decay, disease, deterioration, sickness, complaints, ailments, grievances, blackness, nothingness, disasters, catastrophes and tragedies). Women in the past did not have today's socially acceptable outlets for their voyeurism, as males did. In the 1940's males could not only observe catastrophes, accidents, war scenes, and operations, but act in them as doctors, firemen, policemen, movie projectionists and ushers, and soldiers. Today women have outlets for both observation and action. Theoretically, this offers more opportunity for the resolution of voyeuristic pathology, such as that mentioned by Fenichel (9), where curiosity in women was reduced from action to observation. Unfortunately, it also opens the way for increased pathology in both sexes with the opportunity for more unreduced active sadistic castration tendencies.

Extreme pathological examples of anal voyeurs are found in the early literature (6,25) on the study of sexuality, that is, people who frequent toilets or latrines to study their contents, cesspool and cistern clean-up men, and those who work in funeral parlors or in cemeteries handling the dead. Some examples of negative voyeurs include those who only look for the most sadistic and destructive occurrences in their reading, the proofreader who only looks for errors, the critic who is paid to criticize.

THE DIAGNOSTICIAN AND THERAPIST AS NEGATIVE VOYEURS

The diagnostic situation is one that lends itself to looking for negative aspects and therefore reactivates the voyeuristic-exhibitionistic problem of childhood. The examiner (looker) and the patient (exhibitor)* both bring into the situation a long history of handling their partial instinctual needs. Such situations can never be completely objective. The reason for the referral, and the working situation of the examiner, often play an important role in the voyeuristic-exhibitionistic continuum (why, by whom, for whom). The examiner should be secure enough and free enough of unconscious conflict not to be concerned merely with pointing out the many faults exhibited by the patient. Looking to impress a referring person, senior or supervising therapist at the expense of the patient is indicative of unresolved problems in the examiner. All kinds of sibling transferences and the most complicated of family dynamics are relived in the testing situation.

The examiner must tell it as he sees it, but his "seeing" it is often both selective and subject to many autistic distortions (countertransference) in a negative voyeuristic direction. Searching to get something on the patient (sibling), on the referring party (parent), or to prove somebody wrong are frequent dynamics that must be met in the testing and therapeutic situations. Schafer (36) points out the importance of the overevaluation and underevaluation of the psychological (responses and reports) in terms of the examiner's sense of ego autonomy. The examiner must free himself of unconscious voyeuristic (and other personal) conflicts as the testing situation is so charged that the present is in constant touch with the distant past. The tester is a "psychological voyeur" (36) who peeps, looks at, and sees into the innards of his patient with the saintly sanction of society. The patient's conflict involves whether to reveal and expose himself to the voyeuristic diagnostician or therapist as a passive victim, or to fight against these passive needs. This situation, as mentioned, is supercharged and can cause various reactions of anxiety and guilt in both parties which, in turn, can lead to many further complex transference and countertransference reactions.

Schafer (36) points out that the vocational choice of "psychologist" (and one can add "psychotherapist") is probably particularly attractive to people with an uncertain sense of personal identity who wish to look at and discredit a wide variety of personal identity solutions, either to reassure themselves of their own normality or the acceptability of their abnormality. Schafer (36) says,

*Schafer (36) rightly points out that it would be incorrect to regard the patient as a psychological exhibitionist since the testing situation is often not spontaneously sought out by the patient. The process of self-exposure is not relished, and the patient's attitude is more often one of being peeked at rather than willingly showing.

"Even if the tester did not to begin with, choose testing in part as a more or less sublimated outlet for his infantile voyeuristic inclinations, these inclinations may well seize on the looking-in-secret aspects of testing and thus may invade the professional role." Voyeuristic-exhibitionistic needs, and defenses against them, undoubtedly play an important role in the choice of psychology, psychiatry and social work as a profession. Unquestionably, there are those among us with strong sadistic leanings, who use our profession as a means of belittling, humiliating and controlling others while extolling their own importance, and those who use their psychological reports to expose and destroy.

Everything that has been said above about the diagnostic situation certainly pertains to the therapeutic situation in that the therapist is also in a voyeuristic position. True, the psychotherapist uses no measuring instruments such as tests or stop watches, and he may be very passive (sit in back of the patient and ask for questions) but the patient is quite aware of the voyeuristic-exhibitionistic implications of the situation and eventually lives out the past problems involving these instincts in the transference. There is some material natural to the therapeutic situation which may have anal implications, such as scheduling appointments (regularity), payment of fees (giving), or arranging time. How patients keep their appointments or pay their fees is intimately related to their anality and its particular type. Therapists may allow themselves to be manipulated when not aware of these implications.

Note-taking with certain patients may suggest negative voyeurism, writing down everything bad about them, and therapists who write too often give this impression. When patients stop talking to let the therapist catch up to them with his note-taking, or say to the therapist, "That's important, write that down," it becomes apparent that the patient is using the note-taking in an exhibitionistic and/or sadistic manner. Patients often say to the therapist, "Don't write that down," implying it is bad or dirty. Little Hans when he first commented to his father, who was Little Hans' therapist, about his note-taking, was told by his father that he took notes to discuss the material with Herr Professor Freud. Hans then wanted to know if his father had discussed with the professor Hans' fantasy of seeing his mother naked and noticing her widdler (15). After that, Hans would remind his father to tell this or that to "the professor." Before this point in Hans' therapy, the father, friendly to Freud, who was the therapist of Hans' mother, had been looking for and collecting sexual material on Hans (Freud had asked his patients to do this).

Patients accuse the therapist of thinking bad things about them, of looking at them with hatred, or talking about them to others, and the therapist must be very aware of his own unconscious problems in order to cope with the patient's negative exhibitionistic problems. Therapists who haven't resolved their own partial instinctual problems either unconsciously steer patients away from or towards these problems.

THE NEGATIVE VOYEUR AS PATIENT

The question must be raised as to what is normal negative voyeurism? All people have complaints, symptoms, ailments, dissatisfactions, or unhappiness, therapists as well as patients; these are part of life. However, where the negativism appears to go above and beyond the call of duty, where it is a constant in a person's behavior, (a way of life), where unconscious pleasure seems involved in looking for the negative, hurting the other person or attention repeatedly sought by displaying wounds or injustices, we usually have a negative-voyeuristic problem. As all of us have gone through an anal stage, we all have some anal character traits. However, the degree and intensity of the problem is really what concerns us. Our negative voyeurism becomes a problem when it interferes with our lives or the lives of those around us. The critic may do just fine on his job, but when he comes home and assumes the same role in the family, he's in trouble. The lawyer may impress a large audience with his ability to find all kinds of faults with his opposition's reasoning, but when he practices this technique at home, putting everyone else in the witness chair, the home audience does not appreciate his efforts. However, this too can become a way of life. If members of his family wish to please him, they may do so by giving him the food he unconsciously appears to be seeking. They can become negative exhibitionists. Sometimes such voyeuristic men marry exhibitionistic women (or vice-versa) and have children who perpetuate the voyeuristic-exhibitionistic, sadomasochistic conflict. Consciously, we all want what is good, positive, healthy and the like, but the unconscious message may be altogether different. The unconscious nature of the problem makes it difficult for the patient to see what he is doing, and often such a patient comes in with an interpersonal problem involving not being able to get along with those who are close, with a complete lack of insight and an innocence about it all. Sometimes the patients are children who cannot adjust, sometimes parents enter therapy as so-called secondary patients with no awareness that their child's negative exhibitionism may be related to the parents' negative voyeurism.

The patient whose libido flows into looking for negative things about others, constantly complaining, or the patient who looks for dirt or dust everywhere, can become difficult to deal with, as the symptoms are often ego-syntonic. Such patients make therapists into the anal mother or father and wish to please therapists by their anality, even playing anal sadistic games with them. All other people become obstacles or interferences in the path of this anal seduction. These patients throw their superegos at you ("What's wrong with cleaning the house—don't you?"). If we are aware of what's going on, we can deal with it by appealing to their sense of self (ego-strength) to overrule the superego. We can agree with them and exaggerate the importance of it ("Oh yes, it's most important to keep an absolutely clean house, but you don't seem to have much time for other things"). We must find out what the negative voyeurism or exhibitionism is a defense against before we can do anything about it. Often it is a defense against looking at oneself as feces, as their anal mother or father looked at them in the distant past. They reverse roles and look at everybody else in terms of feces.

The giving up of stools is libidinally invested in relation to another person, and the success or failure of the toilet training process is tied to the nature of the relationship with the trainer. Children do not easily give up their stools unless the preceding relationship with the trainer has been good. The trainer must provide a bridge, as was done when the child was weaned of the bottle or breast.

How the mother or father (dual parenting from the earliest years is quite prevalent today) react to this complicated process is of crucial importance and related to their prior experiences and conflicts. How they feel toward the product, whether it is too much, too little or just right, whether the child takes too long or too short a period of time to comply, and the meaning of time, is of great importance in the development of the child's sense of self. Some mothers or fathers are very voyeuristic, asking all kinds of questions and preoccupied with the toilet and other functions of their child. The mother and father take away and interfere with a private and secret process and offer themselves as a bridge. The child fantasizes about what is inside (part of) and what is outside (comes out) and fears what will happen to the product in particular and the self in general. A part of the body is torn or pinched off, gotten rid of in a violent, explosive and sadistic manner, and this may be the basis of or fuse with later castration anxiety.

The element of time is intimately related to the struggle for power, control, and will between the parents and child. The child may wish to please or displease the parents ("I will give it up, do, make, produce, perform; I will do it when I want to and not when I'm told to"). The child may be proud of his product or think it's bad (or he or she is bad) because the mother or father tells the child the product is no good and smells. When the child thinks he is bad, it may be the result of negative voyeurism, which usually will lead to some kind of anal depression.

Kubie (26) discusses the concept, " . . . everything that is not me is dirt." He points out that it is through the process of projection that one begins to believe that others are dirt producing objects, excreta. Thus, the negative voyeur who sees dirt in another person, is projecting the feeling of being dirty ("I am not dirty, you are") as his parent did when he was a child. He is also saying, "You, you are the dirty part of me, I can't stand you" (split).

Some mothers and fathers not only constantly inspect their children, but seem to want more and more from them, like a wholesale flushing-out, never getting enough to satisfy them. Patients may feel that their therapists wish them to give and give and, like their significant familial object, can never be satisfied. Therapists who appear to be constantly looking for dirt (disturbances, intimate details) in their patients, may unconsciously be considered to be negative voyeurs by their patients who either will feed them this kind of material (like little Hans) to win their love, or run from it, because it makes them too anxious.

Some children give what their mothers or fathers want, but this still doesn't satisfy them: the child did not do it at the right time or in the right place. This parent appears to say first, "Give me," and then, "Oh, what a disgusting product, flush it away quickly," or "Don't touch it, it's disgusting." Such a mother or father is very hard to please because of the inconsistency of their behavior. They both want and do not want, simultaneously love and hate the product (object). It is interesting that Spitz (37) stressed the extreme inconsistency in the mothers of children who engaged in autoerotic fecal play. Patients may feel they do not know what the therapist wants from them and often rightly so. Therapists may wish patients to produce material, then point out what is wrong with it. Children identify with what they produce and wish to please. They use foul language, do foul things, and the message often means, "What's the use, I'm no good." They also say, "I know you don't think much of me, but look at me just the same." If they feel the therapist is looking for a negative production, they will give it as perhaps they did to their mother or father. Patients who depreciate themselves, who think nothing of themselves, or feel others smell better (and they stink), will often exhibit themselves most negatively, even disgrace and shame themselves. Therapists may think they do not give enough to patients and feel worthless. Sometimes our superego chides us, we feel we're giving too little so we give too much and overinterpret.

The impulsive, negative, messy and uncontrollable behavior in patients may reflect the anal feeling, "You can't make me do anything," or "If this is what you want, I'll give it to you but good," or "I'm not going to give up anything for anybody." If the therapist happens to have a controlling, autocratic, oracular personality, it is easy for the patient to make a transference from a controlling parental figure. The negative exhibitionism may take the form of withholding or procrastinating or other passive-aggressive or passive-anal behavior.

NEGATIVE VOYEURISM AND NEGATIVE NARCISSISM

The concept of negative narcissism is also very closely related to negative voyeurism and negative exhibitionism. Perhaps one of the most common examples is its presence in men and women who suffer from severe penis envy (castration). These patients will occupy themselves with feelings that they are bad, neglected, deprived and missing something in life. They feel they are not getting enough and either must gobble up everything in sight, eat compulsively, or push the plate away from them. Such patients will not let themselves enjoy their food and whether they eat or starve themselves they must suffer all the time. Their food, or whatever they have or own, is no good, not enough, others have more or better (envy). They can't exhibit a penis so they exhibit their feces. They identify with the product and feel dirty and worthless, often displaying the "back side" of themselves, asking to be spanked by others. They accept punishment in their back side because they are too frightened and ashamed to show their front side. They often exhibit grievances and collect incidents, injustices and complaints (masochism). Complaints are very precious and enjoyed, but these patients pay a heavy toll for their pleasure. They feel they are being mistreated, deprived, and that they are innocent of any provocation, or that they and nobody else is to blame for everything ''bad'' around them (''look at me and no one else''). They refuse to look into themselves to seek the explanation of why they must suffer such humiliations. They accuse others because they are afraid they will be accused, or they take the complete blame for everything so no one else is looked at. If someone else is being punished they will put themselves between punisher and punished. They either refuse to take the witness chair or are constantly in it. They must prove their mistreatment or their guilt, but in either case they do not look at their responsibilities, or the way they treat or react to others. Provoking mistreatment (look at what you did to me) permits them to rationalize their anger, and declaring their guilt makes them feel very noble and martyred.

This negative or anal exhibitionism will often crop up and must be dealt with in therapy. The patient may feel, ''I am not part of this world. I don't want to live. I have nothing to say, to give, to offer you,'' or ''You wouldn't like to hear what I have to say anyway.'' These patients will act out, ''I hate you because you have it all'' (penis, power), or ''You're cock of the walk and I want to be,'' or ''I want you to look at me, hear me, I don't want to listen to you.'' This can be a dangerous time in therapy as patients in this stage attempt to discredit and humiliate their therapists. Acting out may take many forms: 1) overt manifestations of spreading gossip about the therapist as an attempt to belittle and humiliate, attempting to destroy the therapist's reputation 2) involving themselves in a sexual affair to ''show'' the therapist their back side 3) self-destructive attempts, including marital flare-ups, drinking, compulsive eating. Reactions of this type must be related to the transference.

Analysts need to step back and ask, ''Why is the patient telling me this?'' The drives against which the patient is defending, and how they are related to the transference issues in therapy must be considered by the practitioner.

The negative narcissism or bad aspects of the self are often projected onto a child or another person. When this occurs the patient (or analyst) becomes a negative voyeur and finds all kinds of faults with the child or other person. The patient (or analyst) who feels, "I am worthless, a masturbator, abnormal, the world's worst citizen," becomes "My child (or patient) is worthless, a masturbator, crazy." The concept of the "fecal child" in part has its roots in negative narcissism. "You are worthless" is a defense against castration, a projection of "I am worthless." Patients and analysts who utilize these mechanisms often have a split image of their significant objects and identify with their objects' bad aspects. They may take it out on themselves, become secluded, self-destructive, blame themselves and demand punishment.

Negative narcissism in men involves their inability to accept their masculinity and their phallus. The boy must internalize a loving and not smothering, critical, intrusive and rejecting mother, who accepts his masculinity and penis. The internalized father must provide a model with whom he can identify and who accepts the boy's (as well as his own) masculinity. The father also must not be too critical, competitive or rejecting. If the attachment to and identification with the mother is too strong and the father is weak, absent or emasculated, the boy's enjoyment of his phallic potential will be blocked and neurotic symptomatology such as a feminine identification will develop. If mother denigrates the father, men and their masculinity, or the father stresses phallic power, denigrating and abusing the mother, women and femininity, the result will be difficulty in the boy in his identification and castration anxiety. Men can internalize a bad mother or father figure and become like either. The early mother is usually the initial castrator in both sexes as it is customarily her role to give or return love, to indulge or frustrate, to permit or deny the child. Excessive oedipal conflict can also lead to many different types of difficulties. When both mother and father accept their sexuality, and each respects, loves and helps the other with an absence of role difficulty, the male child stands a much greater chance of reaching healthy adulthood.

Negative narcissism in women is the inability of the woman to accept femininity and her feminine organs. It is intimately related to her internalized image of the mother and the acceptance of her femininity by her father. If the girl has identified with a mother's idealization of the phallus, or directly with her father's phallic image, and the concomitant denigration of female organs—and their active and receptive capabilities—the female cannot develop into a healthy woman. Such patients exhibit neurotic difficulties, such as an identification with phallic males, and an inability to enjoy the receptive aspects of femininity. Or, just as pathological, women with negative narcissism may suffer from phobic reactions and an inability to enjoy a healthy and active sexual life. Women may internalize the father's negative narcissism as well as the mother's although it would be more probable that the mother would have a stronger effect.

Women as well as men have castration anxiety and fears about the loss of their femininity, their organs (vagina, clitoris, ovaries, uterus, breasts) and symbols of them. Girls do not need to "accept castration" any more than boys do; women are not castrated men.

We know today that all members of the family of origin can contribute to the negative narcissism of the child and later the adult. This applies to both sexes and to both patients and analysts.

SUMMARY

A brief summary of Freud's position on voyeurism is presented and brought into line with developmental theory. A psychosexual approach to voyeurism is then elaborated and integrated with Freudian and developmental theory. The concept of negative voyeurism is introduced, defined and discussed in detail. Examples of its usage in diagnosis and therapy are presented. The negative voyeur as patient and therapist are analyzed. Finally, negative voyeurism is related to negative narcissism.

BIBLIOGRAPHY

1. Abraham, K. (1913): Restrictions and Transformations of Scoptophilia in Psycho-Neurotics; with Remarks on Analogous Phenomena in Folk Psychology. *Selected Papers,* 2:169-234. New York: Basic Books, 1953.

2. Abraham, K. (1924): A Short Study of the Development of the Libido, viewed in the Light of Mental Disorders. *Selected Papers,* 2:418-501. New York: Basic Books, 1953.

3. Arlow, J.A. (1980): The Revenge Motive in the Primal Scene. J. Amer. Psa. Assn., 28:519-541.

4. Blanck, G. and Blanck, R. (1974): *Ego Psychology: Theory and Practice.* New York: Columbia University Press.

5. Coleman, R.W., Kris, E. and Province, S. (1953): The Studies of Variations of Early Parental Attitudes: A Preliminary Report. *The Psychoanalytic Study of the Child.* 8:20-47. New York: International University Press.

6. Ellis, H. (1936): *Studies in the Psychology of Sex,* Vols. I & II. New York: Random House (The Modern Library).

7. Emch, M. (1944): On "The Need to Know" as Related to Identification and Acting Out. Int. J. Psa., 25:13-19.

8. Fenichel, O. (1937): The Scoptophilic Instinct and Identification. *Collected Papers,* 2:373-400. New York: W.W. Norton and Co., 1953.

9. Fenichel, O. (1945): *The Psychoanalytic Theory of Neurosis.* New York: W.W. Norton and Co.

10. Ferenczi, S. (1952): On the Symbolism of the Head of Medusa. *Selected Papers: Further Contributions to the Theory and Technique of Psychoanalysis.* 2:360. New York: Basic Books, 1952.

11. Fine, R. (1962): *Freud: A Critical Re-Evaluation of his Theories,* New York: David McKay Co., pp. 62-94.

12. Freud, S. (1900): The Interpretation of Dreams. *Standard Edition,* 4/5:1-626. London: Hogarth Press, 1953.

13. Freud, S. (1905): Three Essays on the Theory of Sexuality. *Standard Edition,* 7:125-143. London: Hogarth Press, 1953.

14. Freud, S. (1907): The Sexual Enlightenment of Children. *Collected Papers,* 2:36-44. New York: Basic Books, 1959.

15. Freud, S. (1909a): Analysis of a Phobia in a Five Year Old Boy. *Collected Papers,* 3:149-289. New York: Basic Books, 1959.

16. Freud, S. (1909b): Notes Upon a Case of Obsessional Neurosis. *Collected Papers,* 3:293-383. New York: Basic Books, 1959.

17. Freud, S. (1910): Psychogenic Visual Disturbances According to Psycho-Analytic Conceptions. *Collected Papers,* 2:105-112. New York: Basic Books, 1959.

18. Freud, S. (1914): On Narcissism: An Interpretation. *Collected Papers,* 4:30-59. New York: Basic Books, 1959.

19. Freud, S. (1915): Instincts and their Vicissitudes. *Collected Papers,* 4:60-83. New York: Basic Books, 1959.

20. Freud, S. (1920): Beyond the Pleasure Principle. *Standard Edition,* 18:7-64. London: Hogarth Press, 1956.

21. Freud, S. (1922): Medusa's Head. *Collected Papers,* 5:105-106. New York: Basic Books.

22. Fromm, E. (1973): The Anatomy of Human Destructiveness. New York: Holt, Rinehart and Winston.

23. Hart, H.H. (1951): The Eye in Symbol and Symptom. *The Yearbook of Psychoanalysis,* 6:256-275. New York: International Universities Press.

24. Jarvis, V. (1958): Clinical Observation on the Visual Problem in Reading Disability. *The Psychoanalytic Study of the Child,* 13:451-470. New York: International Universities Press.

25. Krafft-Ebing, R.V. (1939): Psychopathia Sexualis. New York: Pioneer Publications.

26. Kubie, L.S. (1937): The Fantasy of Dirt. Psychoanal. Quart., 6:388-425.

27. Lane, R.C. (1983): The Shark as a Symbol. (Unpublished Paper).

28. Lane, R.C. and Storch, R.S. (1984): The Wish Not to Know: A Fool Cannot be Blamed for his Actions. Current Issues in Psychoanalytic Practice, 1(1):53-71.

29. Lewin, B. (1939): Some Observations on Knowledge, Belief, and the Impulse to Know. Int. J. Psa., 20:426-431.

30. Lewin, B. (1946): Sleep, the Mouth and the Dream Screen. Psychoanal. Quart., 15:419-443.

31. Lewin, B. (1948): Inferences from the Dream Screen. Int. J. Psa., 29:224-431.

32. Lewin, B. (1953): Reconsideration of the Dream Screen. Psychoanal. Quart., 22:174-199.

33. Mahler, M.S. (1968): *On Human Symbiosis and the Vicissitudes of Individuation.* New York: International Universities Press.

34. Mahler, M.S., Pine, F. and Bergman, A. (1975): *The Psychological Birth of the Human Infant: Symbiosis and Individuation.* New York: Basic Books.

35. Myer, W.A. (1979): Clinical Consequences of Chronic Primal Scene Exposure. Psychoanal. Quart., 48:1-25.

36. Schafer, R. (1954): *Psychoanalytic Interpretation in Rorschach Testing: Theory and Application.* New York: Grune & Stratton.

37. Spitz, R.A. (1949): Autoerotism: Some Empirical Findings on three of its Manifestations in the First Year of Life. *The Psychoanalytic Study of the Child,* 3/4:85-120. New York: International Universities Press.

38. Spitz, R.A. (1965): *The First Year of Life: A Psychoanalytic Study of Normal and Deviant Development of Object Relations.* New York: International Universities Press.

39. Strachey, J. (1930): Some Unconscious Factors in Reading. Int. J. Psa., 11:322-331.

40. Winnicott, D.W. (1965): *The Maturational Processes and the Facilitating Environment.* New York: International Universities Press.

41. Winnicott, D.W. (1975): Through Paediatrics to Psycho-Analysis. New York: Basic Books.

A Case of Exhibitionism: Self-Hatred Beneath a Mask

Laura Arens Fuerstein

The main catalyst for writing this paper was the uniqueness of the case under discussion, primarily in terms of its transference, contertransference, and resistance elements. Concomitantly, the challenges presented in dealing with these issues have been unique and, I might add, often difficult.

The title for this paper evolves from my observation of marked consistency in this patient's treatment patterns: whenever his rage and "mask" of being in control of others through his "perversion" was peeled away in treatment, his extreme self-hatred (including ego-fragmentation and infantile terror of castration and annihilation) was almost always revealed.

I shall now present a review of the literature, then the case, and finally the implications for treatment of similarly difficult patients.

Freud describes exhibitionism as a deviation in regard to the sexual aim. It is considered a partial instinct, as it is the passive aspect of scopophilia (to torture or look at). From childhood on, the experience of this passive aim (to be tortured or looked at) is natural to a degree. It only is considered a "perversion" if it becomes a fixation and the sexual act is not carried to intercourse. Freud adds that the compulsion to exhibit is "closely dependent on the castration complex; it is a means of constantly insisting upon the integrity of the subject's own genitals" (Freud, 1905). Included in this discussion is his well known statement that the pervert acts out what the neurotic fantasizes. He further states that the reversal of an active aim such as scopophilia is replaced by the passive aim of the exhibitionism and is then viewed as a defensive maneuver (Freud, 1915).

Fenichel states that exhibitionism remains more narcissistic than any other partial instinct because along with scopophilia, it originates from the sexual aim of looking at oneself. He also expands upon Freud's concept of exhibitionism as reassurance against castration. The exhibitionist is saying unconsciously: 1) "Reassure me that I have a penis by reacting to the sight of it." 2) "Reassure me that you are afraid of my penis, that is, that you fear me; then I do not need to be afraid myself (identification with the aggressor)." 3) The exhibitionistic act is used as a magical gesture meaning "I show you what I wish you could show me." On this last level the unconscious goal of the exhibitionist is to move the intimidated woman to display *her* penis (Fenichel, 1945).

Melitta Sperling focuses on oral fixation as the most important determinant for the origin of exhibitionism and also mentions the exhibitionist's identification with the mother as the lost object. "While castration fear is very apparent in one layer of the unconscious, in another layer his fear is actually that of losing his life because of having been abandoned by his mother" (Sperling, 1947).

Stoller's definition of a "perversion" such as exhibitionism is that it is an erotic form of hatred. Furthermore, according to Stoller, it is a fantasy, primarily motivated by hostility, habitually acted out, and necessary for one's complete satisfaction. The hostility takes form in a revenge fantasy hidden in actions that constitute the perversion and it serves to convert childhood trauma into adult triumph. It must be portrayed as an act of risk-taking to create the greatest excitement (Stoller, 1975).

Miller points out that there is an introjection of the mother's or father's contempt in the perverse individual. One-time natural childhood impulses were reacted to with aversion, disgust, shock, and indignation. As an adult the pervert "constantly reenacts the same drama: a horrified mother is necessary before drive-satisfaction is possible: orgasm . . . can only be achieved in a climate of self-contempt" (Miller, 1981). All the childhood experiences remain closely related to the parents' scornful reactions and this emerges vividly in the transference (Miller, 1981).

In presenting the case of Roy it is difficult to determine where his fantasies overlap with reality. Also, the history has been slightly fictionalized to protect confidentiality.

Roy is an attractive white male in his twenties. He works in business and is married with two children. He has an older brother Dan, who is unmarried.

Roy's childhood was traumatic. He was told that as an infant he was left in a dark closet for several hours by his father because he had been crying too much. Soon afterward his mother demanded that his father leave the house forever, as he did not support the family financially, gambled, and was physically abusive to her. Roy believes that the "closet incident" was the true precipitant of his parents' separation and ultimate divorce.

Roy describes his mother as frequently absent from the home, either working in a low-level white collar capacity or dating men. He and Dan were left in the care of a seductive, castrating grandmother and a harshly disciplining but caring grandfather (who was perhaps the only positive influence in Roy's childhood). They were the maternal grandparents.

Roy's earliest memory (at age three) is a fear that he would fall backwards out of an open window while sitting on a table with his grandparents around him. At five, he was victimized by his peers for his large protruding ears. With no real explanation, his mother had surgery performed to pin them back. Roy recalls going to the hospital, the ether mask over his face, waking up frightened and alone, and looking differently.

One incident occurred around the same time as the surgery. His mother had a lover at the house and Roy walked into the room naked. The man laughed. Roy fantasized that this was because of his own small penis. Several other incidents occurred in latency and adolescence that involved his mother and female friends staying at the house. Roy describes these women as seductive; for example, he would see one partially dressed coming from a shower. He was asked to massage his mother's back as she lay on her bed with her bra off; this also occurred at various times in adolescence. He once entered his mother's room with a bathrobe concealing his erect penis and then suddenly revealed it to her. She screamed, "What are you doing?" He left, feeling rejected and guilty.

His grandmother would frequently scold Roy for masturbating against the footboard of the bed, and yell out, "You'll get sick!" He relates she once played strip poker with him when he was twelve. She lost the game, he began to strip her but his anxiety stopped him (this seems largely a fantasy).

A sado-masochistic relationship seems to have been established between Dan and Roy. Dan beat Roy up often, spit on his food, and had him perform fellatio on him a few times when Roy was prepubertal. Once a maid caught them in the act, but did not report the incident to their mother.

At age twelve Roy made his first exhibitionistic attempt. While riding home in the back seat of a car with his mother and her friend in the front, he removed his bathing suit and masturbated under a towel.

His adolescence and college years are generally described as unhappy. He often felt isolated socially and did not do well academically. He spent a lot of time either at the pool hall or watching television and fantasizing that he would become an actor playing the part of a "macho man." While in college majoring in some field related to drama, he had several homosexual experiences in which he was the active partner. He reports that he never really felt fully involved in these encounters, yet he wonders whether he could ever become an overt homosexual. He also made his first attempt at intercourse in college. It was disappointing. He was with an older woman and he lost his erection.

After graduation, Roy failed at auditions because of his poor self-image. He could not believe enough in his capacity to play out the "strong man" role for which he often auditioned.

His adult exhibitionism was manifested directly following his grandfather's death, though he was never arrested. Roy would be discovered by a woman as he was leaving a public bathroom with his penis out of his pants, or he would masturbate under a towel in his backyard or while at a red light with a woman in the car next to him. He also undressed in an open window when he thought his female neighbor could observe him. Often he describes the women as knowing what he was doing but not becoming hysterical or calling the police. They merely showed their anger by their facial expressions.

Another manifestation of conflict following his grandfather's death was Roy's stomach and back pains. The stomach pains were diagnosed by a physician as stemming from "spastic colon." The back pains had no physical cause.

Roy appears to have only one male friend (a friend from boyhood). His marital sex life is described as "fair," and his wife as "rather prudish," in his terms. He has visited a number of prostitutes and massage parlors in his adult life.

In viewing Roy dynamically the causes and manifestations of his exhibitionism are primary issues. What seems most evident is a very harsh superego, powerful castration anxiety, acute gender identity confusion linked to a deep homosexual conflict, and severe separation anxiety associated with an infantile terror of annihilation and ego-fragmentation. A powerful rage, acted out through the exhibitionism, acts as a defense against these issues, primarily characterized by a "loss of self."

Roy's history suggests that he was probably the recipient of severe oral deprivation from a frustrating, absent, yet over-stimulating mother, and an abandoning father whose own ego functioning seems quite weak.

Kernberg's formulations help to elucidate the dynamic effects of Roy's preoedipal experiences. He states that when a boy's oral-dependent needs are denied, premature development of genital strivings results. These premature genital strivings are colored by fear and reinforce the future oedipal prohibitions against sexual impulses toward the mother; consequently an image of a dangerous, castrating mother develops. Further, the projected pregenital aggression reinforces oedipal fears of the father and of castration anxiety specifically. A consequence of these dynamics is a condensation of pregenital and genital aims under the overwhelming influence of infantile aggression (Kernberg, 1975). To apply these ideas to Roy, his exhibitionism is both direct evidence of this "condensation" and a means of discharge of the pervasive aggression within it.

The absence of Roy's father from infancy on leads to further understanding of his use of exhibitionism as an aggressive defensive weapon against his infantile terror, and of his confused gender identity. Herzog states that boys probably have a great endowment of aggression from birth on and subsequently their need for a positive channeling of it is equally great. Furthermore, every study of post-divorce adjustment validates the greater pathological effect in pre-oedipal boys than in girls. During a marital separation the mother may experience the disintegration of her own healthy defenses, and her libidinal and aggressive impulses are more likely to be centered on the children (Roy's mother's seductiveness provides possible evidence for this). The focus is on the father as the modulator of aggressive drive and fantasy in children, and the evidence suggests that his absence creates an unmodulated situation, particularly severe in the preoedipal boy. Moreover, Abelin and Stoller highlight the father's crucial role in the consolidation of the child's core gender identity and self-image (Cath, Curwitt, Rose, 1982).

Another view of Roy's dynamics is revealed by insight into his father's functioning. His father was a gambler. Roy's identification with an absent figure must be intensified yet distorted (within the realm of idealization); hence, the probability of the son's internalization of the father's dynamics is increased. Some discussion of "the gambler's" dynamics could therefore be useful in furthering understanding of this case. Fenichel states that gambling is an impulse disorder similar to both addiction and perversion (Fenichel, 1945). Greenson describes it as an unconscious effort to regain infantile omnipotence, a distorted oedipal resolution which offers gratification of latent homosexual wishes as well as oral-receptive and oral-sadistic drives (Coltrera, 1983).

Finally, Roy's choice of acting as a profession, and his failure to succeed in auditions sheds more light upon his exhibitionism. Gabbard's discussing "the pervasive narcissistic concerns underlying all of the dynamics of stage fright," facilitates this other aspect of the study of Roy. Gabbard states that in stage fright, separation anxiety is prominent and grows out of the reactivation of the separation-individuation crisis: the specific fear is that the audience will withdraw its admiration or leave, as the child feared his mother would do. Furthermore, pervasive narcissistic concerns underly the dynamics of stage fright. Prominent among these are concerns around self-esteem regulation and self-validation based on the mirroring or idealizing response of the audience, around envy, around fear of destructive greed, and around shame over exhibitionistic pleasure. Finally, Gabbard states, "A popular saying in theatrical circles is: 'You are only as good as your last performance.' This quotation beautifully captures the performer's sense that each time he performs he is seeking to establish anew his worth as a person, not just as a performer, and each moment in the glare of the spotlight carries with it the risk that he will be written off as a failure by an audience whom he perceives as fickle and as unreliable as his own sense of himself" (Gabbard, 1983). To relate this to Roy, the term "analyst" can be substituted for the term "audience" and his acting-out behavior is better understood.

I have seen Roy for approximately five years, with a two-year hiatus within that period. He began with one weekly session and increased to two rather quickly. He has always sat up. His main reason for entering treatment was a wish to control his exhibitionism, particularly to prevent an arrest. During the beginning phase he would sometimes arrive with an erection. Toward the middle of a session he occasionally unzipped his fly. At times he removed his penis from his pants. These actions were interspersed with little talking. When he did verbalize, it was largely in response to my statements such as, "What are you feeling when you do that?" Interestingly, his reply would relate to his *physical* sensation. He might say for example, "I feel my turned on penis." In an effort to increase his self-control, I encouraged him to talk rather than to act out. While he would "obey" and put his penis back in his pants or zip up his fly, he would say he could not achieve this control. He felt if I would allow him to have an orgasm in front of me, his problems would be solved. When I inquired what reaching orgasm in my presence meant he stated, "I guess it shows that you accept me." I noticed that whenever he was becoming preoccupied with his penis, his eyes glazed over, his responses became mechanical, and I often felt he did not really hear me. I thought of the way a murderer might appear before committing his crime, and I began to realize I must have been the symbolic victim in his fantasy.

After about six months of treatment I had to rearrange two sessions for unavoidable reasons. Soon afterward Roy began to discuss seeing a behaviorist, since the temptations to exhibit with me had become too great, and so had the frustrations. He said he needed a woman who would provide him with "control exercises" and concrete solutions. My attempts to help him discuss the feelings of rejection over the rearranged sessions and his lack of gratification were not effective. I also pointed out that during the time he had been seeing me, his loss of control was present only in our sessions; he had not "exhibited" himself in the outside world for the entire time. However, these attempts failed to keep him in treatment.

Two years later Roy contacted me, saying he wished to work with me again, on a deeper level than before. He said he felt desperate now and the behaviorist had not really helped him. He had almost been arrested several times while exposing himself in public during the two-year period. His description of the past therapy experience was sketchy (as was most of his verbalization). He reported that the therapist was a female who gave him "assignments" to help him control himself. For example, if he felt he was about to lose control in public he was to think about something painful. He considered this conditioning unhelpful, as he was not able to overcome the acting-out with any thought process.

The beginning of the second treatment phase repeated much of what had occurred two years before. Roy still came to sessions with an erection which he produced in the bathroom or waiting room by masturbating. He often would not wear underpants and would stimulate himself on the outside of his pants while sitting there. His various erotic fantasies often involved me. There was still a paucity of verbal material.

I began to recognize a pattern in his acting-out in the session. It tended to occur after a failed audition (this was earlier in the treatment). After the two-year interval, when he had acquired a new employment position, the acting-out would occur after an argument with one of the women in his office, when he felt out of control. My vacations also seemed to set off this behavior. A physician once informed Roy that his wife's difficulty in conceiving a child was partly due to the slow motility of his sperm. This was followed by a period of intense acting-out. One of the longest phases of this activity in sessions occurred after a visit from Dan. Roy was reminded of his childhood humiliation at having his food spat on by his brother. All these situations obviously placed Roy in a vulnerable position, as he feared being castrated and out of control.

In the transference I was the castrating, abandoning, and/or frustrating mother, grandmother, brother, or father. Roy seemed to be reversing the controlling role. He tried to startle me with lewd comments or suddenly rose from the chair, moved toward me, then sat down. Later he said he did this to frighten me. The preoedipal rage and hostility were extremely powerful issues which, up to this point in treatment, had prevented any real working alliance to develop.

Several other elements became prominent and repetitious in the treatment: 1) Roy manifested a tremendous focus on his body as opposed to his inner life; a graphic example of this dynamic is the one I presented earlier, in which I said, "What are you feeling?" and he responded with, "My excited penis." Related to this was a great deal of somatization and hypochondriasis which he brought into the sessions.

2) Roy's silence as a resistance was as powerful as his acting-out.

3) In his periods of control when he did talk, issues of ego-fragmentation, depression, self-hatred, castration anxiety, and homosexual panic evolved. Dreams were remembered and reported more consistently at these "verbal" periods. Most of these were very terse but almost always reflected one of the above-mentioned issues. Examples: "I see bloody meat being chopped up," or "I am trapped in a room and see men with hatchets looking in the windows, ready to get me."

4) Roy very rarely spoke about his wife of his own accord, and if I inquired about this he mentioned his reluctance to have her interfere with the relationship he had with me. It became evident that Roy's wife was the symbolic Madonna and I the prostitute, in his splitting of the woman. Another splitting dynamic was revealed through his power struggles with his female colleagues. He viewed them as phallic castrating types who wanted to control him (and he seeks out their punishment at times), and viewed me as the "all-

good'' feeding mother who will protect him. Intermittently I became the embodiment of both aspects of this split. First, he was unconsciously assured of the presence of his penis through his identification with me, the phallic woman; then he was fearful of, and angry at me for having this power, so he defended against the fear and took revenge by attempting to exhibit to me. Finally he felt remorse and begged ''forgiveness'' as the preoedipal boy asks for a hug from the nurturing mother.

While this theoretical understanding was interesting I began to see that improvement was not possible if I solely employed the familiar interventive approaches. For example, an interpretation was often experienced as a powerful phallic device, aimed at his seduction. Concomitantly, any recommendation that he attempt to control himself and talk rather than act upon his feelings seemed to threaten him; silence on my part was often experienced as a withholding weapon. Any of these three reactions by me seemed to trigger his wish to exhibit, or some action related to it.

I soon recognized that I had to employ some primary interventive route before the three mentioned above could be useful in helping Roy control his acting-out, encourage his verbal communication, and ultimate ego growth. I discovered this route through my countertransference. Heimann states that the countertransference is the patient's creation, a part of his personality, and that the emotions evoked in the analyst should be used as a tool of insight into the patient's defenses and conflicts. Then interpretation and working through can ensue more effectively (Heimann, 1950). O'Shaugnessy extends this idea by focusing on the role of projective identification with patients who communicate in a dual transference of words and activities beyond words. This type of patient often renders the analyst impotent by splitting off and projecting his own impotent and anxious self into the analyst, while he remains identified with a sadistic superego forerunner. Only if the analyst can avoid being identified with these projections and acting upon them, can the patient begin to acquire an observing ego and lessen the anxiety and consequent need to act out his predicament. Following this, mutative interpretation can be made which place the patient in a position to experience in his own words a mutative working through process (O'Shaugnessy, 1983).

With these ideas in mind, I began to associate to my feelings in the sessions. I had associations such as: ''This feels like a shoot-out, in which Roy is saying to me, 'One false move and you're dead.' ''

His penis had symbolically become a gun to him which provided him with some fleeting sense of power over me, the victim about to be shot. I recognized that he must have sensed some anxiety in me in my relating to him, which further gratified his wish to control me. He was rendering me less effective through my identification with his projections of impotence and anxiety.

Stoller states that the lifelong risk for the "pervert" is not arrest, bur rather the persistence of childhood castration/humiliation. "Therefore, the woman who is shocked, who becomes angry, and best of all, frightened, who creates a fuss . . . proves that he has reversed the childhood situation" (Stoller, 1975).

From this point (about a year after Roy's return to treatment), some major shifts began to occur. This new phase began after my summer vacation. Roy presented the following dream:

> A garbage truck is moving down the street past two houses that explode. There are people behind me observing the explosion. In another scene my wife is with an unknown man and I leave. Then there is a party held by an Indian man who says "Think backward." The Indian leaves the party and I follow him, after saying that I need to think forward, not backward.

Roy associated as follows:

> The garbage truck is me; the explosion is my anger, destroying my family (two houses symbolize making the explosion doubly effective); the people behind me observing the explosion are my family and you; I give my wife over to another man because I feel like garbage; the Indian is a mystical figure, probably you, having me look at my painful past which I would rather avoid at times; the Indian leaving the party must refer to your vacation and leaving me.

Immediately after presenting this dream Roy began to touch his fly, and began to speak of masturbating in front of me. I said very calmly, "You must want me to watch you explode as you did in the dream." He smiled and stopped his action. He then proceeded to talk about his feeling like garbage as a child when he had surgery, and about wanting to destroy his mother at that time.

Another evidence of Roy's gratification through provoking fear came after he missed a session due to a vacation. He had not reminded me of this absence in the preceding session. I left a message on his answering machine, asking where he was for that hour. After he returned and received my message, he called and said, "I hope I didn't alarm you."

Related to my heightened awareness of the importance of remaining calm with Roy during his exhibitionistic attempts, was my incorporating more humor in my interventions. Increasing Roy's capacity to laugh with me served two functions: It diminished the strength of his fantasy of alarming me, and it made me a more benign superego figure.

With the reward of alarming me dissipated, Roy began to control more of his acting-out. With a greater capacity to verbalize, his observing ego expanded and his behavior became gradually more ego-alien. Other approaches which helped him confront the acting-out are defined by Bellak as: 1) predicting which circumstances will probably trigger his loss of control again 2) connecting the events or feelings evoked in the previous session with those of the present one (Bellak, Faithorn, 1981).

Now we could begin to explore the self-hatred beneath the exhibitionistic mask. I approached this task in several ways. Sperling states that in the therapy of perversion the analyst's goal is to establish a split in the patient's superego (the split is between the part of the superego that supports the perversion and the part that is alien to it). The perversion-supporting aspect of the superego is harsh and is linked to the child's preoedipal experience when omnipotent parents overwhelmed him with commands that were never integrated. The patient's identification with the analyst supports the aspect of the superego which is alien to the perversion (Sperling, 1956). Strachey describes the analyst as the benign auxiliary superego with whom this identification discussed by Sperling can occur (Strachey, 1934). Furthermore, Fine states that through the expansion of the libido the analyst presents himself as a superego figure different from the parents. The analyst is more accepting of the patient's instinctual drives. Fine emphasizes the importance of the analyst's use of four-letter words to help break down the harsh superego image which the patient projects onto the analyst. Also, as the analyst points out when concealed wishes are evident in the material, or demonstrates a direct interest in the patient's sexual activity, the benign superego image is further developed (Fine, 1982).

I used the above concepts in my technique and this appeared to further the process of breaking down defenses, particularly denial and projection. The self-hatred began to emerge more vividly than before, in dreams and expressions of panic and anxiety during periods preceding separation (before my vacations). Furthermore, Roy became progressively more able to verbalize his anger at me rather than act it out.

Countertransference reactions are always a tool in helping the analyst formulate interventions, and are probably more so with this type of patient. Interventions which involve confrontation, clarification, interpretation, and/or outright recommendations to control the acting-out were not effective in the early stages of treatment without extensive use of contertransference insights. The manner and timing of the interpretation, when one is given, is as important, if not more important, than the wording employed. The analyst must be especially careful not to identify with the patient's split-off, projected feelings of impotence.

Once the excessive acting-out is under control, the analyst can proceed toward helping the patient confront the underlying escape from panic and pain which the acting-out has provided. This task is approached while the control of acting-out is maintained through further use of the countertransference, prediction of circumstances that will trigger the behavior, and expansion of the observing ego by linking past sessions to present ones. Furthermore, the analyst's acting as a benign auxiliary superego figure encourages positive identification, expansion of the libido and ultimate dissipation of the harsh superego. As a consequence, the strengthening of the ego and working alliance can more effectively be achieved. Then, in the words of O'Shaugnessy, mutative interpretations can be made which place the patient in a position to experience in his own words a mutative working through process. I quote a recent statement of Roy's which exemplifies this achievement:

> Throughout therapy I seem to act as if I am facing two doors. When I enter the one, I throw away the keys and exhibit to get further away from myself and my fears, and in the long run get nowhere; when I enter the other, I get closer to myself and my pain but there is hope for another kind of journey.

BIBLIOGRAPHY

Bellak, Leopold, and Faithorn, Peri, *Crises and Special Problems in Psychoanalysis and Psychotherapy,* Brunner/Mazel, New York, 1981.

Cath, Stanley H., Gurwitt, Alan R., and Ross, John Munder, *Father and Child,* Little, Brown and Co., Boston, 1982.

Coltrera, Joseph, Book Review of *Explorations in Psychoanalysis* by Greenson, JAPA, vol. 31, no.3:715-730, 1983.
Fenichel, Otto, *The Psychoanalytic Theory of Neurosis,* W.W. Norton & Co., New York, 1945.
Fine, Reuben, *The Healing of the Mind,* The Free Press, New York, 1982.
Freud, Sigmund, *The Standard Edition of the Complete Psychological Works of Sigmund Freud,* James Strachey, (ed.), Hogarth Press and Institute of Psychoanalysis. a) *Instincts and their Vicissitudes,* vol.14, 1915. b) *Three Essays on the Theory of Sexuality,* vol.7, 1905.
Gabbard, Glen O., ''Further Contributions to the Understanding of Stage Fright: Narcissistic Issues,'' JAPA, vol.31, no.2: 423-441, 1983.
Heimann, Paula, ''On Countertransference,'' 1950, in Robert Langs, (ed.), *Classics in Psychoanalytic Technique,* Jason Aronson, New York, 1981.
Kernberg, Otto, *Borderline Conditions and Pathological Narcissism,* Jason Aronson, New York, 1975.
Miller, Alice. *Prisoners of Childhood,* Basic Books, Inc., New York, 1981.
O'Shaugnessy, Edna, ''Words and Working Through,'' *IJP,* vol.64, no.3:281-89, 1983.
Sperling, Melitta, ''The Analysis of an Exhibitionist,'' *IJP,* vol.28: 32-45, 1947.
Sperling, Otto, ''Psychodynamics of Group Perversion,'' PQ, vol.25: 56-65, 1956.
Stoller, Robert, *Perversion The Erotic Form of Hatred,* Pantheon Books, New York, 1975.
Strachey, James, ''The Nature of the Therapeutic Action of Psychoanalysis,'' 1934, in Robert Langs, (ed.), *Classics in Psychoanalytic Technique,* Jason Aronson, New York, 1981.

Abbreviations:
IJP = International Journal of Psychoanalysis
JAPA = Journal of the American Psychoanalytic Association
PQ = Psychoanalytic Quarterly

Sex and Exclusivity

Judith R. Felton

Although there is a growing body of writing which chronicles the sexual attitudes and behaviors of individuals who engage in the "alternative lifestyles" of extramarital sex, sexually open marriage, and group sex (also referred to as "swinging"), few investigations have presented these relationships from a psychoanalytic point of view. Fried (1972), Felton (1979, 1984), and Strean (1980) have questioned the omission in the literature. However, with the exception of Felton's presentation of some of the most important psychodynamics and intrapsychic constellations regarding sexually open relations, and Strean's (1980) extensive presentation of the neurotic conflicts in the extramarital affair, little has been written in the psychoanalytic literature with a specific emphasis on these particular expressions of sexuality.

According to the data half of all marriages have been reported as exclusive (Ramey, 1976), and extramarital sexuality among both women and men approaches a rate of 50% (Kinsey et al., 1948, 1953; Athanasiou et al., 1970; Hunt, 1974). Also, while an estimated ten million people were engaging in group sex at the beginning of the 1970s (Bartell, 1971), the National Center for Health Statistics (1979) records greater numbers of marriages. And magazines report a return to the popularity of the traditional wedding with all the trimmings.

Psychoanalysts and psychoanalytic psychotherapists are in a unique position to begin to understand the unconscious determinants of these behaviors. Not only do many of their analysands and patients come to psychoanalytic treatment with problems in love (Fine, 1971), but also no fewer than 60% have been reported to engage in

Judith R. Felton is on the faculty of the New York Center for Psychoanalytic Training and the Institute for Psychoanalysis and Psychotherapy of New Jersey. She is a member of the Board of Directors of the Society for Psychoanalytic Training and Director of its Social Science Program. Her practice is in Princeton, New Jersey.

extramarital sexual behavior (Beck and Jones, 1973). In addition, one survey has shown that 40% of the therapists (not necessarily psychoanalysts or psychoanalytic psychotherapists) have engaged in extramarital sexual behavior (Hymer and Rubin, 1982).[1]

This paper is an attempt to build on earlier work (Felton, 1979, 1984) with the exploration of the transference and countertransference considerations related to sex and exclusivity. Earlier work by Strean (1980) has investigated the major psychodynamics of women and men involved in extramarital sexual relationships, while Felton (1979, 1984) has offered a psychoanalytic explanation for sexually open relations. Both have suggested the relevance of the professionals' response, but neither has focused on transference and countertransference implications for the therapeutic relationship.

DEFINITIONS

Extramarital sex, sexually open relations, and group sex (also referred to as "swinging") have been previously described as alternative lifestyles, but require finer definition. Also, sexual and nonsexual extramarital involvements have been previously investigated because of their potential for marital conflict, but they require description. First, however, exclusivity must be explained.

Exclusivity refers to the inclination to exclude other relationships from the primary or marital relationship. For example, a marriage may be monogamous but not exclusive. Monogamy refers to marriage with one person at a time, while exclusivity is related to the degree to which others are excluded in the primary relationship. Therefore, a sexually exclusive relationship, a term which can include a marriage, is one in which there is an implicit agreement that neither of the partners will have outside relationships (Adams and Rubin, 1984).

It cannot be assumed, however, that persons who overtly maintain the traditional convention of sexual exclusiveness are in fact always "faithful" (Rubin, 1982, p. 103). One or both members of a couple who are publicly exclusive may actually engage in sex with another partner on a covert basis. This is defined as extramarital sex.

---

[1]Such a figure appears to be a reasonable estimation for psychoanalytic psychotherapists and psychoanalysts, based on this author's nineteen years of clinical experience.

The sexually open relationship is the term applied when sexual relations with persons outside the primary relationship are acceptable. "Openness," with its emphasis on authenticity in relationships, came to the fore in the 1960s with the growth of the human potential movement, and was specifically applied to marriages by George and Nena O'Neill (1972). Their definition said open marriage is one with role flexibility, extensive communication between the spouses, and an egalitarian lifestyle for married couples. What the O'Neills did not expect, however, was that the term would be increasingly used to connote sexual openness (1977).

Group sex, or "swinging," refers to a sexually open relationship involving sexual relations between a couple and at least one other individual (Bartell, 1971). In group sex, couples always participate together and avoid emotional attachment to reduce the threat to the primary relationship (Felton, 1984).

Some researchers have argued for a broader and more inclusive overview of the area of exclusivity (Weis and Slosnerick, 1981; Felton, 1983) contending that a concept which includes only sexual situations of extramarital involvement is too limited. Not only extramarital sexual involvements, but also same-sex and cross-sex friendships, and relationships in the work environment, are subjects for investigation.

It is also noted that the relationship of homosexuality to exclusivity is unexamined in the literature. For example, while Eisenbud's recent contribution (1982) to psychoanalysis on the determinants of Lesbian choice includes both intrapsychic factors and political context, this valuable paper does not mention problems in exclusive *vs.* multiple homosexual relations.

PSYCHODYNAMIC VIEW VS. VALUES OR IDEOLOGY

It is not unusual for researchers in the social and psychological sciences to have participated in the phenomena which they describe and investigate. Talese (1980) was a participant-observer in his own project about sexuality, and others who have written about controversial sexual behaviors have selectively and discreetly informed others of their experiences, although they have not done so in their published works. It is striking, however, that the degree to which their experiences have been positive is reflected in their work. For example, Bartell (1971) who was strongly involved in the group sex network at the time of his research was knowledgeable about the positive and negative aspects of swinging (Bartell, 1971). He also evoked the criticism of devoted swingers because he cautioned that the major deficit of group sex is the emphasis on mechanical interaction rather than "an intimacy of relations." This deficit, he believed, "reflects the impersonalization as well as the depersonalization of human relationships in our culture." His final wish was for a freedom of sexuality where "human relationships rather than the sexual relationships become the primary goal" (Bartell, 1971, p. 292).

It may be impossible to investigate exclusivity in a completely objective way without bias. Despite an attempt at scientific inquiry, psychodynamic and value or ideological issues are not so easily separated as one might prefer. Superego influences may be reflected in the severity or rigidity of the approach to the subject, without the awareness of the investigator. At the same time, arguments for the expression of impulse without restraint may also be influenced by forces beyond the control or consciousness of the author.

PSYCHOANALYTIC RATIONALE

Because highly individual and multiple factors are determinants for the preference of exclusive as compared with multiple relationships, caution is required in the diagnosis of pathology (Felton, 1979, 1984). Regardless of pathology, however, a theoretical understanding based on the psychoanalytic literature requires review.

The best explanations of the problem and arguments which refute the proponents of nonexclusive sexual relationships come from Freud (1912), Fenichel (1945), Binstock (1973), Kernberg (1976), and Strean (1980). It is Freud (1908) who suggests the most cogent argument for sexual openness. Also, Gediman (1975) is nonjudgmental when she highlights a developmental aspect of nonexclusivity.

Freud (1912) concludes that although civilization's curb upon love and sensual pleasure leads to the debasement of sexual objects and the lack of full satisfaction in marital sexual pleasure, unrestricted sexual freedom from the outset is not much better. Fenichel (1945), too, seems reconciled to the impossibility of adjusting "the claims of the sexual instinct to the demands of civilization." He comments on both the neurotic problem of the restless flight from object to object in the search for gratification in love, as well as the neurotic fear of any change in the love object.

Binstock (1973) states that the intimacy of the adult heterosexual couple resolves the problem created by the mother-infant intimacy. Both, he says, are rooted in physiological need and both to the closest possible psychological relationship. In both, he continues, there are "manifestations of the urge to merge" (p. 94) evoking the fantasy of highest bliss and the ultimate terror—the fear of annihilation.

Kernberg (1976) describes the prerequisites and characteristics for mature love, noting that the achievement of a capacity of depth in relation to one's own self as well as to others creates an interesting and curious counterpart. That is, this process may enable one to find others who could serve as a satisfactory or even better partner. Thus, emotional maturity does not guarantee the couple's staying together. To quote Kernberg:

> A deep commitment . . . will enrich and protect the stability of the relationship, but, if self-knowledge and self-awareness are deep, at the cost of activating from time to time a longing for other relations . . . and repeated renunciations. But longing and renunciation also may add a dimension of depth to the life of the individual and the couple . . . and may bring an additional, obscure, and complex dimension to it. All human relationships must end, and the threat of loss . . . of death is greatest where love has most depth; awareness of this also deepens love. (p. 238)

Strean's thesis (1980) is that when psychosocial tasks are resolved, one will enjoy an exclusive marriage. Although he excuses an occasional "one-night stand" or brief affair as harmless regression, and adamantly views a prolonged extramarital affair as a sign of neurosis, he clarifies that any behavior requires thorough psychoanalytic understanding. If the brief encounters were indicative of compulsive need he would view it as no healthier than an extended conflictual extramarital affair.

Freud (1908) suggests the most cogent psychoanalytic argument against sexual exclusivity, which he called "monogamy." He deprecated the rule against sexual intercourse outside marriage because it led to "modern nervous illness": he was particularly incensed about the lack of adequate measures for birth control; and he was concerned about the culture's barriers to women's sexual curiosity. Such barriers, he believed, frightened women away from intellectual curiosity as well as sexual interest. The restrictive attitude toward sensuality, he held, was also a factor in impotence and frigidity.

Gediman (1975) highlights the developmental transformations related to certain yearnings such as the quest for variety in love. She acknowledges that a number of highly creative people require variety in either the stimulus and/or the love object, along with a need for idealization. Her citations from the literature are combined with her own observation that such longings may relate to an unusual sensitivity to sensory and kinesthetic stimulations from the second year of life. This is the psychodynamic rationale for Knapp's research findings (1976) in which people in sexually open relationships were characterized as future-oriented, imaginative, and risk-taking individualists.

TRANSFERENCE ISSUES

Intra-analytic transference refers to the relationship of the current treatment to the unconscious patterns of feelings and behavior originally experienced with significant figures of childhood. This is of major significance in the analytic process. Its demonstration, interpretation, and resolution are the basis for the therapy. The particular types of transference issues related to sex and exclusivity are important because the technique of psychoanalysis is designed to encourage the patient's regression and the transfer of past feelings and attitudes onto the person of the analyst. Because clinical psychoanalysis depends on the formation and resolution of the transference neurosis as an "artificial treatment illness" (Blum, 1983, p. 588), the delineation of some of its major manifestations of exclusivity are useful.

In one analysand, a professor and scholar, sexual repression of her erotic desires for both of her parents played a part in her attempt to deny her feelings and fantasies about the analyst. The initial consultation was marked by a "testing" of the analyst's stance on bisexuality and multiple relationships. She felt this to be necessary since she was maintaining a long-term heterosexual commitment with the man with whom she was living and also seeing other men. The patient also felt insufficiently understood and was displeased because her previous therapist dismissed the area of sexuality with intellectual reassurance.

As the analysis progressed, Dr. M. continued to meet with men friends and enjoy sexual encounters. However, just as she was beginning to work through a work inhibition, she developed first one and then later another intense and passionate affair with a woman. Despite my interpretation that these were related to our own relationship, and the patient's acknowledgment of such a possibility, her agreement was both intellectual and skeptical. She vacillated between the perception that I was warning her not to become enamored with me, and that I was giving her permission to enhance herself in this way. Because she believed these involvements to be central to her self-acceptance and the working through of her perception of herself as a "failed man," she was preoccupied with her patterns in each love affair. At the same time, Dr. M.'s major symptom, her work inhibition, gave way slowly. Her style of relating to me remained highly articulate, rational, and predominately positive and affectionate. As described by Stein (1981), the transference neurosis was powerfully defended in the patient, who appeared very mature, and had a history of having been a brilliant, charming, and precocious child.

Continuous analysis of the patient's re-enactment of her patterns with her two lovers led to a greater intregration of emotional and intellectual aspects of her experience. Each of her lovers bore a striking resemblance to her two sisters, one of whom was unconventional and the other suffering with illness.

Finally, a breakthrough in our relationship occurred after the patient had decided that, in order to meet her work deadlines, she would have to discontinue her extra-relationship involvements. Previous superego difficulties were expressed by her wishes to avoid sessions when she was unable to write. But she now arrived eagerly with descriptions of her new perspectives in her specialty. As she had once sought her father's approval for excellence in work, she now sought mine. As she had in childhood spent many hours encouraged and tutored by her devoted mother, she now felt supported by me.

As I began to suggest her avoidance of intimacy with the man with whom she was living, she grew furious with me. She envied his professional success and power with women and acknowledged her resistance to him. She was unable to become passionate about him as she had with women, and her excitement for him was induced only by the idea that he was in love with her. Fantasies during intercourse were about women and girls from her adolescence. But when I interpreted these as related to her fears of closeness with a man, she felt as misunderstood and denied by me as by her previous therapist. She experienced relief when these transference interpretations were empathically understood as similar to the times when her mother (toward whom she experienced erotic desire) abandoned her and encouraged her love toward her father. While Dr. M. respected and at times envied or idealized her successful father, she also feared him and felt contempt for his overly flirtatious and underprotective behavior in the area of sexuality.

The patient's repression of her anger toward her mother for masochistically deferring to her father, and for denigrating her own talents and attractiveness, became more conscious—as did her anger toward her father for intruding on her privacy and making her dependent by insisting on financial assistance. She was angry at me for not satisfying her erotic needs, while at the same time she was appreciative that I was a helpful role model, particularly with regard to work. She protected her privacy with me, as with her father, by a highly intellectualized style and the use of words to obscure her feelings about me. She maintained a distance from me and protected her autonomy from the beginning by limiting the frequency of sessions even at times when she was highly anxious. Just as she feared submission to her male lover, she feared that her wishes for merger and the satisfaction of her erotic yearnings would put her in a position in which she felt dominated and exploited by me.

Thus, through the above clinical example some of the major transference issues in the area of sex and exclusivity have been emphasized. The fear of loss of love, Oedipal conflicts, negative Oedipal strivings, penis envy, and wishes for merger at a pre-Oedipal level were in evidence. Narcissistic defenses against healthy love precluded the full development of her sexuality and led to the inhibition of her sexual fantasy life. Finally, problems in self-esteem and the patient's self representation motivated the patient's preoccupation with female lovers as objects of identification and merger. As action outside of the treatment relationship began to diminish, these conflicts began to unfold in the intra-analytic transference. Emotional experience and fantasies and feelings about the analyst increased in order to make possible the required analysis of the transference neurosis.

COUNTERTRANSFERENCE ISSUES

Countertransference refers to the attitudes and feelings, only partly conscious, of the analyst toward the patient. The comprehensive definition (Racker, 1968) comprises all of the emotional responses evoked in the analyst by the patient. In addition, Jacobs (1983) included emotional reactions that color the perception of the patient, regardless of their source. Following these definitions, this refers to both the intrapsychic constellations of the analyst and her or his perceptions of events or experiences of individuals and events known to both the patient and the analyst. This can include political, social, and cultural events, as well as individuals or groups, of whom both have knowledge.

In the case of Dr. M. two countertransference issues were relevant. Her work inhibition was somewhat similar to one from my own past, which led me to be too eager for her to resolve it, particularly at the beginning of the analysis. Although my own inhibition was resolved, the patient's anxiety stimulated my own anxiety, and provoked a need to put a stop to it. Her wishes to avoid sessions early in the analysis were possibly a result of her rebellion against my eagerness, as well as her projection of her standards onto me. Although the patient at first studiously took responsibility for such behavior by revealing her projection of her own standards onto me, awareness of my countertransference problem deepened her analysis. Insight into my own overinterpretation from impatience led me to be more silent about her work and more interested in her childhood and other areas of her life.

A second countertransference stemmed from my research interest in the area of exclusivity and sex. At one point in the treatment, Dr. M. became angry at me for being more interested in the implications of her case for a broad understanding of feminine psychology and sexuality. When I acknowledged empathically that her criticism was well founded, she proceeded to relate the intensity of her reaction to her relations with both her father and her male lover.

Envy and the tendency to avoid her own development while assisting the man in the attainment of his success were central themes. She had fantasied my using her in my writings on feminine psychology and found herself going out of her way to comment on psychoanalytic books with which we were both familiar. Nevertheless, she also criticized herself for being like her mother who avoided developing her own intellectual capacities to care for her family and husband. At the beginning of the analysis, I tended to be too active in probing the work inhibition. However, as the work inhibition subsided, my research interest led me to be induced by her narcissistic wishes. When Dr. M. criticized me for exploitation, reminiscent of her father's and lover's, she was not entirely incorrect. Such understanding then led to a phase in the analysis in which the repression of her wishes for merger and her erotic desires for both her mother and myself were considered. This has been resulting in less criticism of her mother, and a reduced need to devalue herself and her work.

SUMMARY

This paper is an attempt to build on earlier work by Felton (1979, 1984) and Strean (1980) with the exploration of transference and countertransference considerations in the area of sex and exclusivity. Exclusivity, the inclination to exclude other relationships from the primary relationship, is the inclusive term for types of extrarelationship involvement such as extramarital sex, sexually open relations, and group sex.

The problem of objectivity in an investigation of exclusivity is exacerbated because of the influence of values and personal ideology. Theoretical underpinnings from the psychoanalytic literature are reviewed in order to assist the clinician in separating countertransference issues of values or ideology from intrapsychic constellations. Finally, some major transference and countertransference issues are suggested through the presentation of a case illustration.

REFERENCES

Adams, J. and Rubin, A. (1984). "Outcomes of Sexually Open Marriages: A Five Year Follow-Up." Unpublished Paper.

Athanasiou, R., Shaver, P., and Tavris, C. (1970). "Sex." *Psychology Today,* July 1970, 4: 39-52.

Bartell, G. (1971). *Group Sex: A Scientist's Eyewitness Report on the American Way of Swinging.* New York: Wyden Books.

Beck, D. and Jones, M. (1973). *Progress in Family Problems.* New York: Family Service Association of America.

Binstock, W. (1973). "On the Two Forms of Intimacy." *Journal of the American Psychoanalytic Association,* 21: 93-107.

Blum, H. (1983). "The Position and Value of Extratransference Interpretation." *Journal of the American Psychoanalytic Association,* 31: 587-617.
Eisenbud, R. (1982). "Early and Later Determinants of Lesbian Choice." *The Psychoanalytic Review,* 69: 85-109.
Felton, J. (1979). "Sexually Open Relations: A Psychoanalytic Perspective." Presented April 1979, Annual Symposium of The New York Center for Psychoanalytic Training.
Felton, J. (1983). *Exclusivity In Women: A Research Study of Attitudes Toward Extrarelationship Involvement,* Rutgers University Graduate School of Arts and Sciences Ph.D. Dissertation. Ann Arbor, Michigan: University Microfilms, A Xerox Company.
Felton, J. (1984). "A Psychoanalytic Perspective On Sexually Open Relations." *The Psychoanalytic Review,* in press.
Fenichel, O. (1945). *The Psychoanalytic Theory of Neurosis.* New York: Norton.
Fine, R. (1971). *The Healing of the Mind.* New York: David McKay.
Freud, S. (1908). " 'Civilized' Sexual Morality and Modern Nervous Illness." In J. Strachey (Ed.). *Standard Edition (1959) Volume 9.* London: Hogarth Press.
Freud, S. (1912). "On the Universal Tendency to Debasement in the Sphere of Love." In J. Strachey (Ed.). *Standard Edition (1959) Volume 11.* London: Hogarth Press.
Fried, E. (1972). "Marriage In Flux—How and Why?" A Review of G. Neubeck (Ed.), *Extramarital Relations.* In *Contemporary Psychology* 17: 7.
Gediman, H. (1975). "Reflections on Romanticism, Narcissism, and Creativity." *Journal of the American Psychoanalytic Association,* 23: 407-423.
Hunt, M. (1974). *Sexual Behavior in the 1970s.* New York: Dell.
Hymer, S. and Rubin, A. (1982). "Alternative Lifestyle Clients—Therapists Attitudes and Clinical Experiences." *Small Group Behavior,* 13: 532-541.
Jacobs, T. (1983). "The Analyst and the Patient's Object World: Notes on an Aspect of Countertransference." *Journal of the American Psychoanalytic Association,* 31: 619-642.
Kernberg, O. (1976). "Mature Love: Prerequisites and Characteristics." In *Object-Relations Theory and Clinical Psychoanalysis.* New York: Jason Aronson.
Kinsey, A., Pomeroy, W., and Martin, C. (1948). *Sexual Behavior in the Human Male.* Philadelphia: W. B. Saunders.
Kinsey, A., Pomeroy, W., Martin, C., and Gebhard, P. (1953). *Sexual Behavior in the Human Female.* Philadelphia: W. B. Saunders.
Knapp, J. (1976). "An Exploratory Study of Seventeen Sexually Open Marriages," *Journal of Sex Research,* 12: 206-219.
National Center for Health Statistics (1979). In *Hammond Almanac 1983.* Maplewood, New Jersey: Hammond Almanac, Inc.
O'Neill, N. and G. (1972). *Open Marriage.* New York: M. Evans.
O'Neill, N. (1977). *The Marriage Premise.* New York: M. Evans.
Racker, H. (1968). *Transference and Counter-Transference.* New York: International Universities Press.
Ramey, J. (1976). *Intimate Friendships.* Englewood Cliffs, New Jersey: Prentice-Hall.
Rubin, A. (1982). "Sexually Open versus Sexually Exclusive Marriage: A Comparison of Dyadic Adjustment." *Alternative Lifestyles,* 5: 101-108.
Stein, M. (1981). "The Unobjectionable Part of the Transference." *Journal of the American Psychoanalytic Association,* 29: 869-892.
Strean, H. (1980). *The Extramarital Affair.* New Jersey: The Free Press.
Talese, G. (1980). *Thy Neighbor's Wife.* New York: Doubleday.
Weis, D. and Slosnerick, D. (1981). "Attitudes Toward Sexual and Nonsexual Extramarital Involvements Among a Sample of College Students." *Journal of Marriage and the Family,* 43: 349-358.

Essay Review of Herbert Strean's *The Sexual Dimension*

Polly Condit

As I was reading Herbert Strean's newest book, *The Sexual Dimension,* I found myself responding not only to his clear and cogent explanations of human sexuality but perhaps even more to his lively and moving descriptions and explorations of the therapeutic relationship. The questions of what really goes on between the two people in the consultation room, how they experience one another, how one leads the way for the other in the search for self-understanding and emotional growth, how they each learn and grow from the relationship—these are questions not infrequently raised in the literature of psychoanalysis and psychotherapy. The answers, however, tend to be vague and are often skirted or lost altogether in the midst of technical terminology and analytic phraseology.

Anyone who has known Dr. Strean from working with him or reading his previous works knows that he could not discuss sexuality as a separate clinical entity but rather that he would view a sexual problem as just one piece of a far more complex and infinitely more interesting picture—that of the total human being. He discusses sexuality clearly and concisely as he focuses on the psychosexual tasks of the child at each period of his development, looks at the role of sexuality in the adult in all stages and circumstances of life, and explores the sexual underpinnings of psychological problems not usually seen as sexual. Most importantly, however, he discusses how sexual difficulties, both manifest and latent, can be treated psychodynamically. He makes a plea for understanding sexual problems as he understands all human problems, not in behavioral, mechanistic terms but as part of the individual's constellation of fantasies, wishes, fears, conflicts, personal history, and interpersonal relations. He is particularly interested in how the dynamics of the sexual problem unfold in the treatment relationship, and how the person can then be helped.

As he explores these issues through the use of frequent case examples, Strean goes far towards capturing the essence of what goes on in the therapeutic encounter, particularly of the "human dimension" of that encounter. Precisely because Strean does not separate the understanding of sexual conflicts from understanding the rest of a person's psyche, he has written not only a book on psychotherapy of sexual problems but, even more, a book on dynamic psychotherapy. His views about the way people are helped through the therapeutic process are perhaps more clearly illustrated here than in any of his previous works. His discussion of the sexual dimension moves easily and meaningfully into discussions of psychotherapeutic technique. Throughout the book he also demonstrates his ideas of the analytic or therapeutic attitude he believes essential in understanding and working with people.

I would like to try to crystallize out some of Strean's points which I think are so powerfully presented in this book, and are representative of his thinking and teaching about psychotherapy. The major theme that runs through his book is the importance of the relationship between the patient and the therapist, i.e., the understanding and use of transference. Strean describes how to let transference develop unencumbered by inappropriate activity on the part of the therapist and how to use transference to help the patient really know himself on a deep emotional level. Sometimes this work simply enables a very frightened, angry, or suspicious person to stay in the treatment relationship, no mean feat with many prospective patients. He demonstrates how the repetitive themes of the patient's relationships throughout his life will reappear in the relationship with the therapist, and how the patient can then be helped to see these conflicts as he re-experiences them with his therapist. He discusses simple, essential, and yet often not well understood activities of the therapist, such as how to ask questions and when and how to say something. He shows how the person's problems become alive in the consultation room through the developing transference. A particularly important theme in his illustrations is the judicious use of silence to create a supportive environment in which the client can feel safe and understood. Related to this are many examples of how the therapist can refrain from fighting with a provocative person, and meet those provocations with understanding which will lead to the patient being able to wonder why he needs to fight and then to an exploration of his projections and introjections which have made him feel so weak and vulnerable. Another point not often discussed in the literature is which part of the patient's conflict to address. Strean states clearly that the patient must be helped to look first at the fears lying behind the symptom. A case example shows how an exhibitionist needed first to look at his fears and conflicts about homosexuality against which the exhibitionism was a defense.

In all of his discussions of transference, the most important theme that comes through is how to use the transference to keep the therapy an alive, feeling process rather than an intellectual exercise for patient and therapist alike. Psychoanalysis is often accused of being too intellectual and removed from feeling. Analysts are quick to dismiss many patients as not being suitable for analysis. Social workers and other mental health practitioners are also guilty of creating all kinds of categories of "unreachables" and "untreatables." What Strean conveys here is that it is the transference which, if understood and utilized correctly, keeps the therapy in the realm of feelings and true insight rather than arid intellectualizations. It is also the transference which enables many people, dismissed too easily by clinicians, to be helped by dynamic psychotherapy. What Strean says about transference is not new, but how he applies it is the very special contribution he makes to the field of mental health.

It is very arduous work that we do as therapists. We cannot fight, be inattentive, give advice, skip around, give up, talk too much or too little. We must be both observer and participant as we constantly monitor our own feelings in order to be able to understand the deeper levels of what our patients are telling us. The problems countertransference reactions can cause probably cannot be better illustrated than when patients are talking of sexual difficulties. Sex is a topic laden with conflict. Anger is easier to talk about. In many books on psychotherapeutic technique there is little mention of sexual problems. In the writings on more severely disturbed patients, sexuality is often not discussed at all as a theoretical or technical issue. Strean does the opposite. He sees sexual conflict as a part of almost every difficulty, and illustrates repeatedly the way sexual problems can come to light in the therapy if the therapist can listen and allow the material to come forth. He emphasizes how important it is that we understand our own sexual feelings and how often we may subtly stop the material due to our own anxiety. The work of the therapist is most certainly a derivative of his or her own early sexual concerns. We must have enough sexual curiosity and voyeuristic tendencies to keep us interested in the endless details of others' lives. We may very likely have oedipal rescue fantasies. We undoubtedly played an important libidinal role in our families. The nature of our work means that we must continually confront anew our own deepest conflicts from our earliest history, and the reason we became therapists in the first place stems from those same conflicts, and our wish to rework them. When we find ourselves being seductive, inattentive, sadistic, manipulative, or rejecting we must look to our own sexual conflicts which are being stimulated by the patient's material.

It is one thing to maintain the analytic attitude with "analytic" patients, but Strean is unwavering in his insistence that this attitude can and must be maintained with every patient. It is so tempting to resort to other forms of treatment when the patient is resistant, provocative, or engaging in behavior which makes the therapist anxious. Sending the patient for sex therapy when sexual problems are brought up, switching the patient from individual to family or group, deciding that the patient needs directives and advice or sending him for medication are usually countertransference manifestations of the therapist's anxiety about the material presented. Strean insists on keeping his ear tuned into the patient's unconscious no matter which is overtly occurring in the treatment. His respect for and faith in the process of dynamic treatment is evident in every case example. He teaches mental health workers in all settings how to use psychoanalytic principles in their work. He provides a lesson for psychoanalysts who can be too easily dissuaded from their principles when confronted with a difficult situation.

In previous works and in this book, Strean makes the statement that a repetitive chronic complaint is an unconscious wish. This point illustrates well several other ideas which Strean emphasizes. First, as always, one must listen carefully to the unconscious message in the material the person is presenting. A chronic complaint can lead the therapist in the wrong direction. Secondly, if the therapist listens long enough and doesn't interfere with the developing transference, the patient will eventually make similar complaints about the therapist. From there, patient and therapist can begin to explore why the patient needs to have the important people in his life be a certain way. Then the underlying fears and conflicts which the complaints are covering up can be revealed. Strean's classic example of this is the man who complains of his sexually unresponsive wife but who really needs a cold wife because he feels so inadequate and is so afraid of his own sexual feelings. Strean elaborates this theme showing how, as the person is able to feel the same feelings in the transference that he does in his marriage, he can then begin to look at his unconscious conflicts. Strean carries this idea to working with parents of children who are having difficulties. Chronic complaints about the child, if explored, will reveal that the parent has some need, based on childhood conflicts of his own, to have his child express the same problem. As with couples, Strean looks at the unconscious relationship between them and then shows how it emerges in the relationship with the therapist where it is then accessible.

The meaning of complaints has not been explored, to my knowledge, in the psychoanalytic literature, but any repeated communication to the therapist is of great significance. When a person complains, he is trying to tell us something but also trying to hide something. Strean has not elaborated on the dynamics of the "chronic complaint is wish" idea, but we can infer that a cluster of defences is at work. We can see projection of forbidden feelings, i.e., "I'm not afraid of sex, you are." There is also denial of one's own role in the problem and repression of sexual feelings. The difficulty in acknowledging one's fears and taking responsibility for them leads to complaining.

I have referred throughout this essay to how Strean brings psychoanalytic thinking to a variety of treatment situations. Since psychoanalytic concepts are based on the study of the unconscious, they should be applicable to all of us. But so often they are overlooked or considered invalid when treatment is taking place outside of the analyst's room. In this book, Strean takes us into school guidance offices, child guidance clinics, probation offices, social agencies, and an Army mental health facility. He shows us treatment vignettes of violent young children, delinquent adolescents, a prostitute, and the elderly. Though most of his examples are more traditional, his conviction that the same principles of treatment apply with every person and can be maintained in any setting are most poignantly illustrated here. His approach is not a rigid analytic one. He describes very creative work in the therapy of a young unmarried mother of five children. In this case, he discusses the importance of the father in the girl's psychosexual development and then explores the unmarried mother's problems as stemming from conflicted relationships with father and mother. This young woman was treated jointly by a female and a male therapist. The treatments of a delinquent and violent child and teenager are used to describe Strean's views that the "psychopath," far from being without guilt, has in fact an extremely severe superego which has been erected against powerful, frustrated libidinal feelings. Strean recognizes the antisocial behavior as a defense against the painful superego and the obnoxious behavior as a defense against yearnings for love, felt to be unattainable. These case illustrations show how the therapist, armed with this knowledge, can handle the provocations in such a way that the client can gradually let himself feel and express his libidinal wishes to the therapist.

Perhaps because these cases present problems not usually seen in individual treatment, they portray most vividly Strean's principles of understanding each person in terms of his unique psychosexual development, his unconscious, and his current reality. Then, no matter what parameters there may be in the treatment due to the person's special needs, no matter how difficult or obstinate his problem may seem, he must be given the opportunity to develop a relationship with his therapist in which he can re-experience old hurts and fears, and then be able to have a new experience with another human being as they understand the conflicts together. This book which is about the dynamics and therapy of sexual problems really demonstrates that all psychodynamically oriented therapists are good sex therapists, and that good sex therapy is good therapy.